FINALLY

© 2024 Baruani Eustache Ndume

All rights reserved. No portion of this book may be reproduced in any form without permission from the publisher, except as permitted by copyright law.
For permissions email b.ndume2015@gmail.com

Finally by Baruani Eustache Ndume
ISBN: 978-1-0370-2371-2 (print)
ISBN: 978-1-0370-2372-9 (e-book)

Self-published by Baruani Eustache Ndume
Front Cover Art: Desireé le Roux
Cover Design: Anna Krielen
Editor: Zelda Mycroft

Although the author has made every effort to ensure that the information in this book was correct at press time, the author does not assume and hereby disclaims any liability to any party for any loss, damage or disruption caused by errors or omissions, whether such errors or omissions result from negligence, accident or any other cause.

ABOUT THE AUTHOR

Baruani Eustache Ndume was born in the 1990s in a small village named Lubomo in the South Kivu Province of the Democratic Republic of Congo. When he was seven he fled the DRC to escape the violence that civil war brought and returned twenty-three years later, having spent most of this time away as a refugee in Tanzania.

Baruani is an internationally recognised children's rights activist having been awarded the International Children's Peace Prize in 2009 (aged sixteen) for leading a movement that reunited over fifty refugee children with their families through the radio programme he presented which was broadcast in all the refugee camps and surrounding towns across Eastern Africa.

He recently reclaimed his DRC citizenship and is currently pursuing tertiary studies in Cape Town, South Africa. He believes that he can work alongside others to bring about change in the world and education, for himself and others, is the key to unlocking these opportunities. He continues to advocate for all children, in South Africa and elsewhere in Africa and the rest of the world.

Baruani believes that all children, irrespective of race, nationality, religion and culture deserve the same rights and should be respected and honoured. As a social leader and international activist he continuously advocates for child-driven leadership.

After more than two decades of living in a refugee camp he is now free, a legal citizen and ready to embrace this new chapter in his life.

Finally!

b.ndume2015@gmail.com

*Thank you to everyone who has been part of this journey:
my family, friends, supervisors, mentors.*

It would have been impossible to travel through these seasons alone, without your support. I really appreciate it and respect your efforts. I am forever thankful.

CHAPTER 1

LIFE BEFORE THE WAR

My life before the war was good.

The village of Lubomo is situated on the Ubwari coast among other villages. People from these villages only had farming and fishing as their daily activities, with men and women involved in farming and men also fishing. Those two things kept village life going; there were no activities other than farming and fishing.

Our villages had small churches and mosques. There were two tribes living in Lubomo at that time: the Bembe and Bwari tribes. I'm not sure of the exact number of people in my village at that time. Our village had no fence or registration process in order to know how many people were coming in and leaving. People would arrive and leave the village while others would settle and after a few months they would move to the next village. Things we did not have and I still find unacceptable is that many villages in my homeland, the Democratic Republic of Congo, had no schools for kids to go and learn to read and write. At that time almost seventy percent of villages in the DRC had no schools. Some villages had a school for Grades 1 to 3 only, so in order for a child to continue to the next grade families were forced to move to the next village, or two or three villages away, to find a school presenting classes for Grades 4 to 6. So often there were simply no schools. If your parents wanted you to go to a high school they would have to make sure they had enough food and money to pay for you, which was far more expensive compared to living in the smaller villages. People were very poor and having to relocate to a big village where there is high school was a sacrifice made by the entire family. We had this same big challenge in our village: we had no school which is why at the age of seven I had never been to school. I didn't know that school existed. I only knew about going to the farms to work. I couldn't even write my name. That was in 1999.

I was only able to attend school to learn how to read and write when I was nine. But I'm getting ahead of myself ...

Let me tell you about my family. There were just three of us in our home: my mother, brother and me. My dad passed away after a short illness when I was about five or six years old - I don't really recall what the problem was. My father was Msewa and my mother's name was Sifa; my brother was Swedi.

But first let me tell you more about what happened to my dad. From what I can gather at that time in the village his sickness was not normal - his illness did not last very long; in less than six months my dad's condition deteriorated. We had no hospitals in the village and our only 'hospital' was the traditional healer. With the support of other villagers my dad was taken to different traditional healers and they all said my dad died of poisoned food that had been given to him by a witch in his dream. In spite of being born into a Christian family we all believed this explanation because we were also raised in these beliefs of witchcraft and super natural powers. Traditional healers were our only guides and we believed that they were helping people. As part of the tradition children were not allowed to go see sick people when they were being treated and I therefore never said goodbye to my dad. In less than six months he was gone. I had no idea what was going on. Swedi and I were not informed of how he was doing because it was our cultural tradition not to involve children in these adult conversations.

This was a most difficult time for my mom to support us because we had no one else to help us except some villagers who assisted with food and other small things. I was confused because I had no one to report to. All my friends had their fathers and I had no one. I felt angry, sad and that life was unfair. Swedi and I were both confused because we were told our dad was travelling and would not be coming back home. This was the way in which our elders explained death of a loved one to children. There was nothing else to ask but it was hard to believe and even harder to live with.

Traditionally, if one of the villagers lost a loved one, a few people would be selected to support them for a period of time. So villagers treated us well during that period. It took us a long time to cope with my father's death and get used to living without him. Even though I was a young boy at the time I felt that something was missing; my family was not complete. But I didn't know what else my mother could do.

A lot changed after my father's death - even the level of respect we received from the villagers. At that time a woman was not recognised as someone who could lead a family, so the disrespect from men in the village towards my mother was quite evident. They conducted family meetings where only men were invited – consequently we had no one to represent our family and my mother was not allowed to attend because she is a woman. In this way our family lost status in the village. We lost our voice with my father's passing.

My mom's role changed completely. She became both father and mother in order to make sure her family moved forward: there was no one to help her, she had to do everything on her own. My dad's name was Mzee Msewa: he was between 30 to 35 years of age when he died.

All the houses in the rural villages in the Democratic Republic of Congo were built with walls made from mud bricks and grass roofs. Every household built its own house by themselves but sometimes some villagers would come and help. All the houses were round in shape. Everyone collected mud and grass for their own house as you were expected to do it for yourself, but sometimes you got lucky and friends and relatives helped. The grass was not specially treated. It was so plentiful that you just walked into the bush and cut whatever kind of grass you found and started building your house or toilet. The houses were not that close together, a few metres apart, and each house was big enough to accommodate the size of the family. Larger families had larger round huts – smaller families had more modest huts. Some plots had two or three houses for the same family, depending on how big the family was. But only married men and women were allowed to have their own houses with all the children sleeping in the house together with the parents.

No electricity. No flushing toilets. No running water or taps. No gardens. Villagers built small toilets and bathrooms using grass from next to the house. We had traditional toilets in the village, each family had one. Toilets were a big hole covered by branches of trees, grass and soil. There was a small hole in which one would poo. When it was full we would dig another one next to it. After relieving yourself you would use water to clean yourself. No toilet paper - just water. We used water from Lake Tanganyika to wash ourselves, wash our clothes and cook, drinking water straight from the lake. At night we used fire to light up the house in order to see while making our beds and doing other chores. Fire plays a major role in village life, traditionally helping villagers cook food, providing light in and outside of the house. And lastly, but most importantly, it is the place where you discuss family matters, sing and dance and have fun as a family. It is the centre of each family and each community.

My mom, Swedi and I lived in our small house alongside other villagers. Lubomo is in the South Kivu region of the Democratic Republic of the Congo. We lived a happy life on the shore of Lake Tanganyika. Lubomo was, and still is, a small village, making it easy for people to know one another. As children the only field we had to play in was the shore of Lake Tanganyika. You could see all the kids playing there from early morning till dusk. Two friends whose names I still remember are Isebo and Debaba. They were our neighbours and we played together most of the time. Isebo and Debaba were my age, we were all seven. We played together all the time, playing around our houses, showering at the lake and playing in the water. None of us attended school so when we got back from the farms we played together. Isebo and Debaba were not brothers – they were neighbours from different families. We were all neighbours together. We also played with kids from other parts of the village, most of the time we played football together. We were all the same: poor families with no education, the only difference was that some children had both parents while others had one. I was happy for them but wished that all of us had both parents. We were not just villagers living in separate homes; we lived together as an extended family. All the villagers were kind to my brother and me.

Anytime we felt like enjoying ourselves, my brother and I would run naked from our house straight to the water and start to play. These memories I will never forget. It was such a special time of my life, having time to play with my younger brother who, in the next few years, I would never see again.

Swedi was two years younger than me. He was quiet, calm and always happy. He liked to play non-stop. He would follow me wherever I went and asked questions over and over again. For example he asked incessant questions: Is this your friend? Where are we going now? Can we carry on playing? He disliked being told he could not go with the older boys, and hated it when we didn't wake him up when he fell asleep. He would cry for hours and hours until he fell asleep again. We often walked together to our small market, eating and fighting all the way! Of course I teased him – he was my brother, after all! When I was doing something differently to the way he wanted it to be, I just smiled! It was so easy to annoy him, but he found it difficult to stay angry with me smiling at him all the time. I tried to teach him valuable things, especially when building our small play houses. These were good moments between brothers who believed in each other.

We were more than best friends because most of the time he was close to me, asking for my help, laughing, having fun through our hours of play. I miss him. Being where I am now, what I miss the most is my brother. I keep imagining what it would be like having a younger brother. Here. Now. How cool would that be? We would be able to talk about everything and help each other in so many ways. I miss him being here, close to me.

I wish now, that I had photos and videos of those fun times - at least that would have helped me gain closure because I could connect with him through these pictures. I can't help thinking now how wonderful it would have been to have a young brother whom I could take care of and encourage to become a gentleman.

There were days we used to accompany our mother to the farm to help her work in the fields. These are the best and most beautiful memories I have of growing up as a child, together with my little family. I will never forget this.

My mother was a queen. While growing up I heard people calling her "Sister Sister". At that time I thought Sister was her real name and I started calling her Sister! People laughed at us because she answered me. Then people started asking: Why are your children calling you Sister? Because you are calling me sister - they are following your lead!

I never knew that "sister" is a term of respect used by women for one another, especially the younger women addressing their elder "sisters". It took a while for me to stop calling her sister and start calling her Mama (mother). My mother treated me with so much care, no matter how poor we were. That is the way our family lived. She used to tell me: you know you are my Tata (father), you are my protector. I felt very proud to be told that because it showed how much she believed in me.

She was a busy woman, very energetic, working and often going to the market to sell her bananas in order for us to survive. I saw my mother as someone who sacrificed herself for the family. She deserves much credit. My mother had unending love for me and Swedi. At this young age I realised there is so much to be said about having both a mother and a father. A parent's love is incomparable, anyone can try their best to love you but they will never beat the love of a parent. I often think about my mother standing shoulder to shoulder with me, supporting me in everything that she thought I was capable of doing.

I miss that. I lost that at such a young age.

I keep trying to remember as much as I can of those early days - even though I was a small boy at the time. No matter how difficult life was, my mother tried to make sure we lived a good life according to the village standards. She was a strong woman.

In the Democratic Republic of Congo, we have approximately two hundred and fifty tribal groups and each tribe has its own language, culture and tradition, even though some cultures and traditions look similar. In the province of South Kivu we have more than ten tribes, one of which is mine. I am Bembe. I am from the Bembe tribe. In our tribe when it comes to marriage a man can marry as many women as he pleases. This is our custom. It is common to see a man with thirty to forty children of his own. I remember one day I asked my mother about her family, where they lived and how many siblings she had. She told me that she came from a big family with her father having three wives and more than ten kids, all of whom were married at the time and living in different villages.

How, you may ask, can one man marry so many wives and have more than a handful of children? Very easily. It is our culture and therefore deemed normal. You are not forced to marry multiple wives but if you want to no one would stop you.

In my culture, at that time, it was not unusual for a girl of twelve to be married to an old man because the family needed money and the only way to get it was through early marriage of young girls to older men. Women were considered to be in waiting - keen to get married and give birth to children – which was viewed to be their core function in the family. In most families only boys attended school. It was thought that only boys were mature enough and smart enough to study. It was thought that girls were simply waiting to get married. And that is that.

As a young child this is what I believed. In some villages many people still believe this. They do not think that girls deserve or are capable of gaining an education. Today I live in a different world with a different world view and I ask myself: Was this right? Does it still happen today? From a different perspective, could it be described as human trafficking?

In the 1990s we had no phones or communication devices and you communicated with friends and family members in a very strange way: through letter writing! You write and if you don't know how to write you ask someone to help you. You then send the letter to a friend or family member through someone who is travelling to that specific village or going in that direction. The trick was to find someone who going to the right village who could give your friend or relative the letter. This involved a high level of trust because you didn't know if the person would deliver the letter or not. Some letters arrived and some did not reach their destination because situations arose that prevented the letter-bearers from delivering their letters. Sometimes it took six months or even a year or more for a letter to reach a friend or loved ones.

Lack of technology and limited transport made it even more difficult to meet in person. It was difficult to keep track of one another and know if your family and friends in a different village were still alive. Very few people in the village had radios, so during football matches you would find people in groups listening to news or listening to football matches on the radio. Everyone imagined what the people looked like but nobody actually knew. We were isolated, living in a world apart, on the outside.

My mother did not know if all her family members were still alive because in order to know where they were she would have to travel to various villages where they lived to check that they were still alive. If they weren't at the nearest village she would have to travel to the next, and the next. If they had moved to a different village she could send a letter with someone who was traveling in that direction. This was a big challenge for people like us who were unable to travel and it resulted in us not knowing family members in person because we never met them. As a result, I am unable to confirm how big the family was both from my mother's side and my father's side as well. I never met any of them because of the difficulties presented by limited communication and transport.

These are the same people whom I later started looking for.

The DRC went through many long wars during the colonial period and after independence in 1960. Those were still days that people in villages were only able to hear news regarding what was happening on the other side of the world through their radios.

Nobody, no matter how poor, or where they lived in small villages, thought that one day the war would come. It was inconceivable that so many would die while others would be separated from their families forever. Villagers like us, living on the other side of the world, were cut off from all news. Bit by bit, story by story, people started hearing that there was war in the country and in some provinces close to our province. Some villagers started asking questions: What are they going to do with us here? We are poor and have nothing of value to offer them. Perhaps they will go to the cities where there are things they can claim? We had nothing and I didn't think they would come this far into the countryside.

My mother was confused and didn't know what to do. She was waiting for the situation to come to an end, hoping that war would not come to our village. Everyone was confused because they weren't getting reliable information, so men in the village were unstable and afraid. Children told stories about our football teams and helped each other on the farms. As a seven-year-old I was scared of dying. At the time I can remember feeling helpless and hopeless: What can we do now, with only three of us? I wished my father was there. He would have found a way forward, a way to avoid what was coming. He would have helped us escape to another village far from where we were staying. If only he were here ...

Villagers did not know that the mission of the rebel soldiers was not to steal but to gain power by killing civilians and raping women and girls. They were ready to do anything in order to achieve this mission.

In 1996 civil war broke out in various areas in the South Kivu Province. People were killed in masses by rebel soldiers. There were no proper communications at this time so it was easy for these rebels to go around and do whatever they wanted to do. Raping women and girls before killing them was commonplace. It was a time of confusion and terror. Everyone was living in fear; we expected anything to happen at any time, not knowing what to do. Some villagers had been in that situation before and lost family members and they were scared to go through it again. Some of them fled our village with the goal of going as far away as possible. The problem was that no one knew where these rebels would come from, so they were confused and fled in a haphazard way. Some of the larger villages housed a thousand people or more. During this time many villages lost ninety percent of their citizens through the savage action of rebel soldiers.

In my village not everyone survived but there were survivors, like me. Many people living in those villages now are new; most of the old villagers did not make it out alive. The survivors all have bad stories to share, especially those who had previously lost relatives. Everyone was scared of war and wanted to live in peace no matter how poor. As a little boy in these turbulent times I felt very anxious because I was in danger. That is not the life I deserved to live. I wanted a happy life but it was impossible and there was nothing I could do about it. Mama always told us not to worry about it, saying nothing would happen to us, we won't die and everyone would be okay. My brother was scared. I felt helpless and could do nothing other than cry and hope for survival for all of us.

In 1999 I was seven years old. The rebels came to our village and broke our families and friends apart. Many people have never been found after this carnage. Some ended up killing themselves after being the only survivor in their family. They felt there was no reason to live if all their relatives were gone. They lost everything. Every member of their family. Gone.

Some people survived.

If you have never experienced such devastation you may think this cannot happen.

But it did happen.

It happened to me.

CHAPTER 2

THE WAR STARTS

Let me tell you about the day rebel soldiers came to our village. The province of South Kivu and the Democratic Republic of Congo in general have endured wars between the government and different groups of rebels from within and outside the country for so many years. Congolese people never enjoyed a life of peace after independence because so many civil armed groups were created. Many groups were, and still are, fighting for power and position in the government. So much created in the DRC was destroyed after independence and peace disappeared. One civil armed group would fight the other, the government and army were fighting one another. Everything was fucked up. This is how civil strife started across our whole country.

On this particular day in 1999 people woke up to an ordinary day, ready to start the day with the usual daily activities. Some villagers were getting ready to go to the farms while others went to the lake waiting for fishermen to arrive so that they could buy some fish and then go sell them in our small market in the village.

It was a bright, sunny morning with the sun newly rising and everyone starting their day. The sky was blue and clear. Beautiful. Villagers knew what time it was, especially at night, with the help of birds. When you hear a particular bird's voice you know it is not yet time to wake up. When you hear the voice of an owl you know it is between 1am to 3am, but when you hear the voice of a cock then you know it is between 4am to 6am and it is time to start getting ready, to get up and go. This is how villagers told time, especially at night. We followed the sounds of the night birds. During the day, particularly in the eastern part of the DRC, villagers would ask you to stand in the sun and, by looking at your shadow, would determine what time it is. A human sun dial. And they would be right every time.

On this particular day everyone in the village was busy; some people were on their way to the farms while others approached the shore to welcome the fishermen home, keen to buy their catch. I could hear the voices of the day birds in the trees and the sound of roosters and hens from our neighbours. Typical morning sounds with everyone awake; even animals were walking towards the shores to drink before making their way to the bush. Where there is a village you will always hear the sounds of children singing and playing. It was a normal day, the kids were up as usual, ready to start the day. Older kids like me were ready to help their parents on the farms or with other chores.

Younger kids started their day playing different kinds of games, as village kids do: playing football, building small houses, singing, dancing and so on. Men and women went about their usual busy day on their way to farms, tending their homes, cleaning and preparing food for their families. It was an average day. I was on the shore with my mom, waiting for fishermen so that she could buy fish to sell at our village market. Swedi, was a short distance away outside our house sitting on a chair, waiting for us to come back so that we could go to the market together. It was a beautiful day.

Suddenly we heard the sounds of guns from the mountains. The time had arrived. We feared that no one was going to survive that day.

I was shocked. It was the first time I'd heard the sound of gunfire. I was confused and did not know what to do so I started to cry and hid my face in my mother's skirt, trying to avoid hearing or seeing what was going on. People started running towards their houses, shouting, calling out names, crying. Mama and I started running as well. Towards our house. Towards Swedi. Before we could get to our home I remember my mother shouting his name, telling him to come to us. When we arrived at home he was not there. My brother's cute, innocent face was nowhere to be seen. We couldn't find him. He wasn't in or around the house. We followed others who were running towards the forest. We didn't know this was the route the rebels had used to enter our village – ambushing us – denying a way to safety. Shooting and shouting voices terrified us – moving ever closer to the village.

People were running in different directions, fleeing to where they thought they would be safe. My mother took my hand and we started running towards our house, towards where we had last seen my younger brother. Both of us were crying. Out of nowhere we found ourselves surrounded by soldiers who were shooting wildly into the air and also at people running from them. They seemed determined to kill everyone in the village.

These rebels were fighting against the government in a bid to win power. Once they entered the village they shot, killed and slaughtered villagers, raped women and girls and doing other inhumane things. To gain control. To gain power. They were dressed in green combat gear and I don't know if it was their combat gear or if they had stolen it from other groups. They were intimidating and made us miserable if we did not comply fast enough with what they wanted. All I could hear was the shouting: big voices celebrating victory while people were dying around them. They were fighting in packs so it was difficult to know how many there were at any one time. All of them had weapons: big guns, short guns, knives. Their tone was threatening. Even in Swahili their voices were menacing, shouting and swearing at the villagers as if we had done something wrong or owed them something and did not want to pay. I was unsure whether they were real soldiers or civilians who had decided to take up arms. All I knew is that they were rebels fighting to gain power.

Some rebel soldiers herded villagers into groups while others set their homes on fire. They took a group of people - men, women and children, all together - into a small house and set the house on fire, making sure they were all dead before continuing to the next home. We could hear the voices of people crying out, asking for help. Help which was impossible to give.

I was in a position of not being able to help and it hurt a lot because I felt that I should have done something to save peoples' lives. I felt guilty. But the reality is that I was helpless. I was traumatised. I was seven.

I couldn't stop crying because I was in a situation where my mother, younger brother and I needed help but no one was there to help us. Everyone with us needed someone to come and help. My mind was stuck; nothing worked. I couldn't think, I couldn't move. I felt as if someone had pushed me from a tall tree and I was plummeting downwards, heading for a big rock. My heart was about to explode. My life was worthless. I didn't deserve to live.

Why was this happening to us?

Is this the reason why I was born into this world?

Was this really happening or was it a nightmare?

Shock. It's hard to explain how I really felt. I was physically alive but psychologically dead. My mind was empty.

We didn't deserve what happened.

It started off as a normal day. Kids were playing outside their houses. Guns approached our village. People ran in terror. Rebels shot at will. Villagers died in the shooting frenzy while others were locked into their homes which were set alight. They died there.

We didn't know what to do, running frantically, aimlessly. As we ran my mother and I were caught by a group of soldiers, forced into a house and told not to make a noise.

Running. Crying. Chaos. Rebels were beating villagers, forcing them into houses. Everyone (including me) was crying loudly for help and forgiveness from the rebels. My mom was asking them to forgive us, asking what we had done wrong. Pleading for them not to kill us. Begging to be forgiven, not knowing what we had done wrong.

Rebels kicked us into a random house. I thought they were just making sure we didn't make a noise or run away. I never knew they were about to set the house on fire with all of us inside.

The flames caught. We could do nothing other than cry and hope for a miracle, a way to escape.

I will never forget that day; afraid of being killed, not knowing what to do, the only child among the villagers in that house.

A lot was going on in my mind but I felt paralysed. I could not believe that something like this could happen to destroy our lives so quickly. I had always been one hundred percent sure that I would be with my family forever - no matter what.

Back inside the burning house people were trying to break the doors, desperately trying to get out. Because of my age and small size my mother managed to push me through a dug-out section under the door and told me to run without waiting for her. She said she would meet me soon. I agreed because I knew she would come. I started running, crying, not knowing where I was going. The soldiers were still there. I didn't know what to do. It was a matter of life and death. I found myself doubting whether to continue or go back.

Those who have been refugees or have faced civil war and invasions will know and understand what happened to me so many years ago.

It was dead quiet.

The sounds that started this day were missing. No laughing. No singing of children. No joyful talking. No birdsong.

The only thing I could hear was the sound of guns popping and people crying. Similar sounds were coming from the other villages. The chaotic noise was all around me and also in the forest where I was running to hide. I stopped crying because I was afraid that the rebels would hear my whimpers and finally kill me.

I continued to run for some hours without stopping, not knowing where to go. Would any place I found myself in be safe?

I asked myself: Where is my brother? Where is Swedi? Where will I find him?

My confusion was overwhelming, not knowing where Swedi and Mama were, wondering if they were still alive, fearing that something bad had happened to them.

I was terrified. I needed help and I yearned for my brother and mother. There was nobody else I trusted. What had happened to them? What would happen to me? How would they know where to find me?

No answers. Crying was not enough to express the anguish I felt. What was going to happen to me?

My life changed in a few chaotic hours. I felt like a dead child even though I was still breathing. I was exhausted after running for hours trying to save my life, something I did not know how to do. Would I make it out alive? And then God sent me an angel.

I did not give up and carried on running for what felt like forever, crying inside, looking for help. After a long time I met an old woman who later became my saviour and helped me escape.

She felt sorry for me. Which village are you from? Let us go this way!

She was shaking and confused, worried about her own family. We did not introduce ourselves to each other, so I didn't know her name, but immediately after we met I started calling her Bibi (Grandma). Instinctively I knew we had both survived a similar trauma. After meeting me Bibi took my hand and we ran together, just the two of us. The terrain was rocky and sandy with small trees across the paths. The forest was not dense enough for wild animals like lions, tigers and elephants to roam. It was a more sparse forest, mostly used by people as a footpath to neighbouring fields; a place of farming and cutting trees to build houses and toilets. This forest was home to smaller animals like chimpanzees, monkeys, deer, squirrels, snakes, birds, rabbits and many different types of insects. With all the shouting and crying, and the sound of guns everywhere, even the animals had gone into hiding.

It seemed as if Bibi knew where she was going. I didn't want to ask at the time and followed quietly and obediently. We ended up in a distant village on Lake Tanganyika where we met a host of people waiting for a boat to carry them across the lake.

We slowly made our way to a neighbouring village. I didn't know where we were going until we arrived in a small village on the shore of the water. As we got closer we could hear people talking to each other. All their faces were new to me, they started talking to each other about the plans for the boat and how to accommodate all of us. What boat? We were waiting for a boat to take us further. They asked about my family and I said I didn't know where they were. They easily understood me and one of them said: We all know we are in this together. Our first goal is to get out of this place then we can decide what to do next.

Every moment I told myself how important it was never to give up. You must never give up. Always be ready. Do not feel that God does not see you. After what happened to me that day I knew God was there and no matter what we were going through he would always be there for me.

I was born into a Christian family so I was taught that everything good that happens is by the grace of God and everything bad that happens is caused by Satan. In that moment, I believed that God was with me and wasn't ready to let me die. It was a difficult time where I had experienced both bad and good experiences simultaneously. Feeling God close made me determined never to give up, no matter the situation.

People from many other villages had fled similar attacks. There were men, women and small kids, everyone showing the trauma of what had just happened, not knowing what to do. I sat there staring at them blankly, with no idea of where we were going. Going back home was not an option so we waited. Waited for a way to escape.

A small boat arrived and we all got in and started crossing the lake. I asked Bibi where we were going. She responded: I will tell you when we get there. We will be back soon, don't worry.

She knew I was confused and to calm me down stopped me from asking so many questions. I understood she was looking out for me so never asked another question.

We journeyed through the whole night in the boat. I did not know where we were going. I thought that maybe we were going to a neighbouring village and would be back soon. Such a small boat normally took about thirty people. There were so many people in the boat that at one point the water started lapping over the sides. I could not move my legs because the boat was so full. This was my first time travelling in a boat.

I was confused, angry and did not know what was happening. Some people were crying, others tried to calm them down. After a while all were silent. Nobody talked. Nobody cried. For hours. I occasionally spoke only to Bibi because everyone around me was fearful, angry and upset.

I vomited the entire journey because of the trauma I had survived and the danger I still felt around me. I knew no one in the boat except the old woman I had met just a few hours ago. Bibi was the only one who knew I was there.

But still somewhere deep inside I was hopeful.

And I waited for my mother to come …

CHAPTER 3

BECOMING A REFUGEE

In the morning we arrived in Kigoma, a city on the shores of Lake Tanganyika, and were taken to a big warehouse while waiting for the next step.

I had no idea what was going on and what the next steps would be. I was there with nothing to do so simply followed instructions and waited. The centre was overflowing with refugees and officers from UNHCR (United Nations High Commissioner for Refugees – the UN Refugee agency)) and other organisations supporting refugees. Tanzanian citizens were not allowed to enter the centre so the only Tanzanians we spoke to were some of the officers who were Tanzanian. The warehouses were full to the brim and people were talking twenty-four hours a day. You could hear noise all the time. Some people slept while others talked, and some cried.

We waited for a few days to be registered as refugees. I did not know what was going on and what it meant to be registered but thought the family I was with would know what to do next. While waiting to be registered people were searching for their loved ones in different cells, in different warehouses. Bibi finally found some of her children and told them about my situation. All of them helped me to look for my mother while waiting to be registered. Sadly, we couldn't find her, and also two of Bibi's family members who were missing.

I was worried about what would come next. At the time the UNHCR was registering families, as family units, processing them as a unit to be moved together to a refugee camp. I had no family and, as a result, Bibi and her family did not want to leave me - a seven-year-old, all alone in this chaos.

I had no option other than to rely on what they thought should be done to help me. It is very hard to be in a situation where your life decisions depend on others. To have no freedom to choose. To hope that those helping you make the right decisions. As desperation consumed me I was ready to follow everything they suggested. It was tough but I had to embrace the assistance they were offering. It was my only option.

After a long discussion as a family, Bibi told me that they had decided to register me as one of her grandsons and that we would travel together until my mother came to fetch me.

I was not consulted, they told me what they had decided. That was it. I had to agree and follow them. That was my only option at that time. And it was a good decision.

I was registered under her missing husband's name and as her daughter's son.

At the time I didn't know where her husband was. I thought that he was maybe dead and apparently so did Bibi. Many years later we discovered that he was still alive when he arrived unexpectedly in our camp. He then passed away much later.

Again Bibi reassured me: You are part of my family now. But when your mother comes then you will go.

I was cool with this because I lived in hope that my mom and my younger brother would find me so that we could continue our lives together. I was okay with it because Bibi was ready to help me and then when my mother found me her responsibility to me would be over.

That's when my identity changed. Instantly. I stopped being Obedi Msewa and became Baruani Ndume in order to prove that I was part of the family with whom I had fled.

It would have been impossible for me to survive had Bibi left me behind with no one to look after me. She allowed me to move on to the next step, to survive. At that time refugees were flooding in, hundreds every day, so I knew my mother would arrive in the refugee camp sometime soon.

I was looking forward to seeing both Mama and Swedi again and hearing what had happened to them and also explain to them what had happened to me and how devastated I felt without them all this while.

It was a long and tedious thing being processed by the UNHCR. First your identity had to be verified. This involved the head of the family providing details of each family member. The next step involved all family members wearing a plastic bracelet with an identification number on it. Then we were told to wait in specific warehouses. There were separate warehouses for men and women and each warehouse accommodated approximately two to three hundred people.

Sometimes when you find yourself in such extreme situations you simply agree to the instructions you're given, even though you don't understand or agree. Nobody said anything, everyone followed instructions. The children stayed with their mothers or guardians. Strangely, even though I was also a child of only seven, I was ordered to sleep in the men's warehouse.

Most of the people came from different provinces in the Democratic Republic of Congo: South Kivu, North Kivu, Maniema, Ituri, and many more districts. All of us spoke Swahili as well as other native languages.

You can imagine how noisy it was in these warehouses with hundreds of people talking and also much non-stop crying. So much noise can give you a headache. The noise was stressful to me because all the stories were about the war; how people had died and survived. I listened to people close by and often became emotional at the sight of children who had their family members there; moms and dads, brothers and sisters. I had no family there. It was tough.

No matter how big the warehouses were we could understand one another through our common understanding of Swahili. Everyone had a different story to share: some had lost their kids, wives, husbands, uncles, and aunties, all of them dying during the war. It was an emotional place where people cried because they felt abandoned and were in mourning and shock. This bothered me a lot because I also felt that pain. It felt as if I was not a human being anymore.

I don't remember exactly how many days we spent at the transit area in Kigoma, but it was no more than three days before we were taken to a refugee camp. One evening a UNHCR staff member arrived and started calling the names of those who would be taken to the refugee camp the next day. Our names were on the list and we started getting ourselves ready for the next morning,

I couldn't sleep. I was stressed. I missed my family. I was exhausted. I decided to be still and wait for what the next day had in store.

Early the next morning we were ready in the waiting area, waiting for our names to be called so that we could climb onto the trucks.

It all felt like a bad dream, a nightmare: being forced to leave my village; crossing Lake Tanganyika in a small boat; arriving in Tanzania, getting a new name; becoming a refugee. Everything had happened so quickly.

I had thought that we would be in Kigoma for a few days then return to our village. I was too young to realise that we were already refugees in Tanzania and there was no chance of going back home to the DRC.

They told me: we will stay here for an unknown period of time until peace is restored in our villages back home. I thought they were telling me we would return back home when that group of rebels was done fighting.

Then I thought: There are so many people here, why don't some of us go and kill those rebel soldiers? Only much later I learnt that it is not about killing all the killers, it's about making sure there is no more fighting and killing ever again. Of anybody. By anybody. Only then would we be able to go home.

I couldn't understand why they wouldn't let me go home. I didn't like the life I was living. When I accepted that there was nothing I could do I realised I had to wait to see what would happen next, where it would all lead. I was a kid who had no control over the decisions being made over my life. I didn't like it but had no power to refuse or go against the adults. I was hurting inside and nobody seemed to notice or care. There was no one interested in listening to me or what I wanted. I wanted to go home, I wanted my mom, I wanted to be back in the only place I had lived since I was born.

I was physically present but not there mentally. I was psychologically traumatised. We were given biscuits and pap with beans but I had no appetite. People kept telling me: Eat young man, we don't want you to die here. You have come such a long way - please force yourself to eat - even a little bit.

So I forced myself to eat a few biscuits and drink some water.

They started calling names. They had previously compiled a full list of families and the names of all the family members. So they called out just the family name (surname) and the head of the family had to step forward to confirm the family members, who were then allowed to climb on the truck. And then the next family name was called …

Things were not going the way I wanted so while waiting to get onto the truck I just looked around at people, waiting for my turn. Most people were impatient, tired and in need of a place to rest.

After waiting two to three hours our family name was called and we climbed up a ladder onto the Iveco truck with the UNHCR sign on the side.

And so our journey as refugees started.

We didn't know which camp we were going to but the driver knew. After being on the road for almost five hours we arrived at a place where all the trucks gathered; a village along the road. We were given thirty minutes to drink some water and relieve ourselves before we continued with the journey. It took us ten hours to get to Lugufu Refugee Camp. Before the arrival of refugees, the place was called Mitamba. The Tanzanian government and UNCHR decided to change the name. No one knew why. At that time there were ten refugee camps in Tanzania: eight Burundian camps and two Congolese camps. The eight camps housing Burundian refugees included Lukole, Mtendeli, Nduta, Kanembwa, Mkugwa, Muyovosi, Mtabila I, and Mtabila II. The two camps housing Congolese refugees were Nyarugusu and Lugufu. Nyarugusu was established in 1996 and Lugufu in 1997. Eventually Lugufu II was established in 2004 and then closed in 2007 when all refugees were moved to Lugufu I.

And so I arrived at Lugufu camp; the year was 1999.

In the beginning we slept in long, big tents while waiting for the UNHCR to allocate each family a more permanent site where we would live. Nobody knew exactly where that would be. UNHCR officers, together with other organisations supporting refugees in Tanzania welcomed us to the Lugufu refugee camp as our new home. That first evening we were given prepared pap (maize porridge) and beans for dinner and water to drink. We slept in huge, communal tents for two days while waiting for UNHCR officers to take us to the place we would be staying permanently. Each family was given plates, pots, spoons, forks, maize flour, beans, cooking oil – all determined according to the size of the family.

I was ready to face a new chapter in my life. The only question I kept asking myself was how would my mom know where I was if we kept moving further away? How would she know where I was?

After waiting a few days our turn arrived. We were taken by UNHCR staff in charge of plots to the address where we would be staying. This time we walked – no trucks. Our plot was approximately fifteen kilometres away; a new camp in a wilderness of bushes. We decided to cut down the bushes with machetes and used the branches to build the frame of a temporary tent while we made plans to build a house. We helped one another to build houses with mud bricks and grass roofs. People stayed in these mud houses for about five years, depending on how strongly the house was built. Sometimes heavy rains could damage these houses, some were destroyed by heavy rains and thunderstorms. We built many houses so that all family members could be comfortable but also have enough space.

Initially, we built four huts to accommodate the family. On the first night we ate pap and beans. I remember this meal well. First we made a circle of three rocks, placed firewood between the rocks, lit the fire and rested the pot on top of the stones. The aunties prepared food for the family. There was no time for fireside stories that first night because everyone was exhausted from the day's walk to reach this place, and working to build the makeshift tents that formed our temporary home. We all ate and then immediately went to sleep.

Many families around us were also busy working at their own new home sites. Nobody helped one another that first day because we were all new and everyone was busy with constructing their own shelters. On this day people talked and laughed while working. A new beginning ...

This is how my life as a refugee started in Kigoma, Tanzania. For my entire life in this camp I stayed with the same family, the Ndume family, sharing four huts. There were thirteen people in total: five children, four parents, one uncle, and two aunties.

And then there was me.

CHAPTER 4

LIFE IN LUGUFU

Lugufu refugee camp was in the Kigoma region in the district of Uvinza, ninety kilometres from the shores of Lake Tanganyika. It was surrounded by the neighbouring villages of Mwamila, Basanza, and Kazaroho.

The camp itself was arranged in Zones, Villages, and Blocks: eight zones, with each zone having four villages and each village having twenty-four blocks. In total Lugufu refugee camp had thirty-two villages.

There were no fences surrounding the camp but the Home Affairs office and Police Station at the camp entrance on the main road was the point of entry. To enter the camp required each visitor to specify the reason for entering the camp. If the authorities determined that your reason was valid you were granted a permit for a specific time. First, you had to report to the home affairs office and then to the police station before entering. The government made sure everything was monitored just in case anything unusual happened. The camp was very big and visitors could get lost. Or maybe fall ill. To get help the authorities needed to know if you were in the camp and, if so, where you were. They would first run your details through the home affairs office to check whether you had entered the camp legally and if you had entered illegally you would be punished according to the law, when they eventually found you.

Refugees were allowed to leave the camp under special circumstances, with certain restrictions. Refugees could leave the camp if they had an important issue that needed to be attended to outside the camp, for example: medical treatment, court issues or other activities allowed by the Tanzania government. If you were allowed to leave the camp Home Affairs would give you a permit, which included your picture, and specified what you were going to do and how long it would take. When you left the camp you had to be accompanied by a Tanzanian citizen who was working in the camp or, if you were allowed to leave alone, you were obliged to report to Home Affairs regularly until your return to the camp.

Each case was processed differently. If you were going for medical treatment Tanzania Red Cross would take you to Home Affairs with all your documents (refugee identification number, passport-size photos) and other relevant documents to confirm that you were a registered refugee. After that Home Affairs issued the permit and determined the expiry date. Leaving the camp for educational purposes involved a similar process with an organisation supporting refugee educational programmes being the agency in charge of assisting refugees to get a permit.

Back in 1999 and still today, refugees do not live amongst Tanzanian citizens. Tanzanians are in their home country and they have all the rights as citizens: freedom to live where they choose; the right to vote; the right to buy land; freedom of movement. This was and still is different for refugees who do not have the right to vote, can't buy land, have no freedom of movement and speech, and are denied other important rights that involve recognising their dignity as human beings.

We had many leaders in Lugufu Camp: camp leaders, zone leaders, village leaders and block leaders and they were all supported by and fell under the guidance of the United Nations High Commission for Refugees (UNHCR) and its partner organisations who supported refugees. Every two years elections were conducted to elect leaders who represented refugees at different levels. They also worked with authorities to support refugees in resolving issues of dissent. Dissent between refugees would first be reported to the village leader, the matter would then be reported at the police station. Police officers worked together with village and zone leaders to maintain peace and harmony in villages. In modern city leadership terms, a village leader could be described as a ward counsellor, a zone leader as the mayor, and the camp leader as the president. These leaders played a big role in maintaining law and order in the camp. All refugees from the age of eighteen participated in electing their leaders. As we all know election drama happens everywhere: some people complained about their votes being 'stolen' because their candidate was 'the perfect candidate' over others who may have won the election. Thankfully these disputes did not result in physical fighting or vandalism. Elections were conducted like any election in modern urban democratic spaces: candidates would be notified when to start their campaigns and they were instructed to respect the election rules which were set by the Ministry of Home Affairs (Refugee Department) in the camp.

The UNHCR worked in partnership with the Tanzanian government through the Ministry of Home Affairs, the Principal Commissioner of Prisons and the Regional Administrative Secretary. NGOs like the World Food Program (WFP), United Nations Children's Fund (UNICEF), Tanzania Water and Environment Sanitation (TWESA), Tanzania Red Cross Society (TRCS), Christian Outreach Relief and Development Diocese of Western Tanganyika on Education, World Vision Tanzania (WVT). The list is endless …

Each organisation supported refugees according to their mandate and they were passionate and committed to making a difference. After a few years they started building schools for refugees, centres were established to help displaced families and gender-based training was provided for refugees and victims.

As a child new to the refugee experience school was the most interesting thing I discovered. I was seven years old when I fled the DRC and had never attended school. In the camp I was able to go to school. I think I was nine when I went to school for the first time.

I was so happy and ready to learn because I dreamed of being a doctor or a teacher. Education at last! We were given books, pens, pencils and sharpeners by UNICEF. There were eighty to a hundred kids in one classroom, often making it difficult to hear or understand the teacher. The classes were full and noisy! There were many older kids like me and the way teachers tested if a child was school ready was to ask you to touch your left ear using your right hand - over the top of your head. No kidding, that's how they determined that you were older than seven!

I started in Grade 1 and for the first time learnt how to read and write. Swahili and French were the languages of tuition in all schools in the camp. There were multiple grades in each school as some older children had started school back in the Congo so they were able to progress to the higher grades.

In the early 2000s there were very few schools in Lugufu and the UNHCR did not build a proper school building for years. Primary and high school students were all studying under the trees. Teachers were not paid so life was very difficult for them. Our teachers were refugees too, many of whom had been teachers in the DRC.

It was difficult to attend school under the trees, studying in an open space with no chairs to sit on and no tables to write on. We sat on bricks during school time. It was disastrous when it was windy because our books were blown away, making writing and studying difficult. I was happy to learn but the environment was a challenge. With all the challenges I started feeling that maybe I wouldn't be able to become a doctor or teacher when I grow up. It took more than three years for the whole school to be built and for all students to be seated at desks in classrooms.

School lessons ran from 7h30 to 13h00. No lunch. Nothing other than water. The principal used a whistle to call students back to class after a break. A whistle also dismissed us at the end of each school day. Parents built temporary classes using grass for the walls and roof so that their children were protected from the sun and rain while studying. The toilets were not great because they were constructed using wood and mud, the same way we had built them back home. Years later World Vision Tanzania, supported by the UNHCR, built proper toilets with sand, cement and bricks. There were no flushing toilets but seats built over holes in the ground.

Teachers used blackboards and wrote with chalk. There were no books for students for many years but teachers had books they used to teach us.

We started each day with singing and then the teacher got to teaching 'normal' subjects. The entire education system in the camp was refugee-driven: refugees who had gone to school and had qualifications helped principals and teachers develop lessons and often became teachers themselves.

The organisations helping with education in the camp reported to the UNHCR office in Dar Es Salaam. It was bizarre that, as DRC refugees living in a camp in Tanzania for Congolese refugees, we had to follow the DRC education system. This meant that when students in Grades 6 and 12 did national exams inspectors from Kinshasa brought DRC exam papers and then returned all the answer scripts back to the Congo to be marked and assessed. They then sent these results back to the camp after a few months. Our education system was complicated.

After a few years of arriving in the camp the UNHCR, through the Christian Outreach Relief and Development Diocese of Western Tanganyika which supported refugees in Education, started building schools with bricks and galvanised roofs. When the school buildings were eventually built we had desks and chairs.

Slowly things started improving: we got books and then, after a few years, school uniforms too. As a refugee you often don't get what you like, at the right time and enough. You may be in a position where you want a uniform but they come and give you books. And then when you need books something different comes along. You accept it all because there is nothing else to do: your family can't help you with the things you need for school so you accept what you get and manage with what you have.

I loved learning! Studying was not easy but it helped me learn to read and write, starting with my name. I had a favourite teacher. I told Teacher Mauridi everything, sharing what had happened to me, from the war until the time I arrived in the camp. He was a father to me, showing me love. In love and gratitude, he gave me his birthday date which I still use to this day: 15 March is our birthday.

I don't know my actual date of birth because my mother never told me what it was and I also had no birth certificate to prove when I was born. This is a huge problem for many refugees, children and adults alike, something that affects us throughout our entire lives. Children like me don't know their real age. There is no way to identify someone when there is no system to trace them. This lack of proof of my identity, date of birth (and therefore my age) was difficult to accept but what choice did I have?

One day Teacher Mauridi came and told me about an organisation that was helping children who had been separated from their relatives, I spoke to Bibi and she told me to go to the office for support. The next morning I went to the office of the International Committee of the Red Cross (ICRC) where they asked for my details: my real name, place of birth, name and surname of the person/s I was looking for. They took a passport-size photo of me in the hope that my family would see it and recognise me. Bibi supported me, making sure everything was okay. A few months went by and Bibi and I went back to the ICRC who told us to come back later as they were still waiting for a report from their team in the Democratic Republic of Congo. They said they would get back to us within a month, when they had information.

They never did.

After Bibi and I reported to them multiple times they told me that they couldn't find my family. They told me that I was not the only one on the waiting list and if they found my family I would be notified.

Nothing.

I was deeply stressed and in pain because I couldn't see a future; I couldn't imagine a life without the hope of being reunited with Mama and Swedi. I knew I had Bibi and her family and I wasn't alone.

But I felt abandoned. It hurt not knowing whether your precious family members were still alive or dead.

Nothing.

This is when Bibi and I knew it was over.

There was no way I would ever find my family.

Maybe with a miracle from God?

CHAPTER 5

BECOMING AN ACTIVIST

In 2007 at the age of fourteen I joined the Child Voice Out Committee. This World Vision Tanzania (WVT) initiative involved young children rolling out the Child Voice Out Programme in their schools. The support I received from WVT through the Child Voice Out Campaign was the fuel that made me fall in love with activism.

I always wanted to do something to support others who had gone through and were still going through what I had survived. I knew there were plenty of kids like me who had not yet been found by their families and needed support. So I signed up for an interview conducted throughout the camp. After the interview, I was among those who were selected to serve on the committee.

The Child Voice Out Committee was made up of three children from each village, twelve kids in each zone, with a total of ninety-six members from thirty-two villages. I was elected as the Committee Chairperson with an additional five members elected as the Executive Committee.

I was the head of all the committees and the one in charge of all the activities, supported by the executive members. Our role was to facilitate communications, develop action plans and run various programmes like school poetry competitions, soccer teams, campaigns on children's rights and gender-based violence. It was our job to make sure all the required activities were properly planned and implemented. The executive committee met every week to prepare and to be briefed by various authorities. It was our duty to provide feedback from the children and communities at large regarding previous activities and plan for the future so that we could share information with the whole committee during the General Assembly. I was happy to be elected to lead this group because I was doing something that I loved and was passionate about; this was my contribution to my community and I was proud to do it efficiently, with the support of my fellow committee members.

I think I was elected as Chairman because I showed publicly that I was passionate about children's rights. My energy levels during the first interview and on the actual day of the election were extreme! I was happy, smiling, confident and yet also very concerned about the challenges affecting refugee children like us inside and outside the camps. All the committee members were boys and girls between the ages of twelve to seventeen years old.

A week after being formed this 96-member committee was renamed the Children's Parliament. Our major function was to conduct child-driven campaigns at schools, interview the most vulnerable children about gender-based violence and other issues negatively affecting them and report our findings through monthly meetings. In short, encouraging children to speak about their challenges.

There were two types of meetings: the Executive Committee meeting and the General Assembly meeting. The Executive meeting was held twice a month before every General Assembly meeting. The General Assembly also met twice a month: at the beginning of the month and at the end of the month. All these meetings, as well as other emergency meetings, were held at the World Vision Tanzania / Child Protection head office. We were allowed to travel freely from village to village within the camp, as long as it was between the curfew times of 04h00 and 22h00. Child protection officers were present at all our meetings. Sometimes we invited special guests from the departments of Health, Education, Gender-Based Violence (GBV) and various other community leaders to speak to us and also to listen to our thoughts regarding various issues that needed their input and action.

GBV was a big issue. Where I came from in the DRC a woman was not deemed to have the same value as a man; a woman was not considered to be an equal human being. Even when it came to education only boys were allowed to go to school, and girls had to stay at home to cook for the family. When they got to thirteen, fourteen or fifteen they were expected to marry, often enduring abuse and violence in their marriages; children married to adult men. This is one reason why GBV workshops and activities formed a big part of our Child Voice Out Programme. One difference in the Tanzanian refugee camps was that parents were forced to send their daughters to school. But old habits and perceptions endured ...

This campaign helped identify many children surviving horrendous trauma and supported them in various ways. One form of support provided by the Children's Parliament involved creating a platform through which children could report these incidents to the authorities and then get appropriate support.

I was very happy to be on this committee because I was part of a team making a positive impact in refugee children's lives. According to the UNHCR almost twenty-five thousand refugees were living in the Lugufu refugee camp at this time.

A year later the time to be more proactive arrived as we wanted to bring as much positive change to refugee children as possible. In 2008 my colleagues and I came up with the beautiful idea of expanding our activism, reaching out on a different level. There was a radio station called Radio Kwizera in the Kagera region, four hundred and twenty-three kilometres from Lugufu. We knew that through the medium of radio we would be able to reach many more people. At the next Children's Parliament meeting we discussed this idea and all the members agreed. The Executive Committee presented our idea to our supervisors, Mr Nabulizi Buloze Matanda and Mr Lweýa Sadiki, who assured us that they would submit our proposal to their head of department, Mrs Edith Pagula, for approval and support. World Vision Tanzania/Child Protection Department agreed to support our radio programme!

In less than three months everything was finalised and we were ready to roll out the next step. World Vision Tanzania reported back to UNICEF and UNICEF was excited to sponsor our radio show in partnership with World Vision Tanzania. It was a go!

This was great news because we could discuss relevant topics of importance on the radio programme - topics which we had been discussing locally through the Children's Parliament. In this way children in refugee camps across the country could learn from what we were discussing. A few days later we were told it had been approved by World Vision Tanzania and UNICEF. The committee and I started to select children from the Children's Parliament who would participate in the radio programme. With the support of Mr Mazibo Kangetha, a journalist from Radio Kwizera, we were ready!

The radio show was called 'Sisi Kwa Sisi' (Children for Children). We prepared our topics and selected those who would participate in each discussion, then rehearsed for two to three days. The Radio Kwizera team brought recording equipment to the camp and we recorded multiple shows. The 'Sisi Kwa Sisi' radio show was on air every Sunday at 17h00 for forty-five minutes.

Some of the topics included fundamental children's rights and responsibilities, education, the right to play, child marriage for girls, the importance of women in leadership, the right to a name and nationality. This radio programme ran for almost eight years, so we had a lot of topics that were discussed during this time.

Through the radio show we reunited over fifty children with their parents in refugee camps across Tanzania. I think one of the reasons I was passionate about the radio show was that I had hope, again, of finding my loved ones. I never did.

Family separation was a big problem for so many refugees. I was very happy for those who were able to reunite with their loved ones. I couldn't imagine how they felt about being together again.

Even today some of my friends have decided to let it go because they were not able to trace their family members.

Through various sports activities and setting up a Children's Parliament we continued to bring young people together, promoting human rights and acceptance of one another.

We needed the participation of all children and wanted to change people's mind set about children's rights. It doesn't matter that you are a child, your rights should be respected and protected. The community in which I was raised believed that when you are a child - a girl or a boy - you don't deserve to be heard. You need to listen and follow what you have been told by the adults, without question. Adults did not believe that a person with a disability could do anything worthwhile or participate in decision-making and disabled children were largely ignored and excluded. Through this program we were able to teach the community to change this belief by including disabled children and give them an opportunity to share their thoughts in decision-making. We had a few disabled members who were part of the committee so through them the community was able to learn and accept that we can all contribute and offer valuable input, irrespective of disability.

Refugees in Lugufu camp came from mainly South Kivu, North Kivu, and Maniema in the Democratic Republic of the Congo. Afternoon activities included playing very basic football, with very few resources. Most of the children in the camps were struggling from trauma after going through difficult situations at an early age so they needed everything possible to help them settle. The UNHCR and the International Committee of the Red Cross helped many to connect with their families living in other villages within the camp - there were many children under UNHCR supervision.

The Children's Parliament, sports, and the radio show had a big impact on children's lives, inside and outside the camps. Because of the impact of the radio show more children wanted to participate in our workshops, trainings, campaigns, and sports competitions. Through all these activities, people started believing in children as future leaders.

We started receiving letters of congratulations and thanks from communities following the 'Sisi Kwa Sisi' radio show. Letters were sent to Radio Kwizera, UNICEF and World Vision Tanzania from families thanking us for the work that we were doing for our fellow children. Their letters were sent to the offices of the various agencies/organisations and officers would read them to us. Sometimes the actual letters were sent with UNHCR officials. This made us feel that we were doing something good for the community.

Some parents also wanted their children to join the teams participating in the radio show. This was difficult because we couldn't include more members on the committees. Our solution was to include more children by alternating who could participate in each radio show, in this way ensuring that everyone who wanted to had a chance to be included. This strategy was welcomed because it included more children.

We always thanked our communities in the camp and neighbouring villages who were listening to our radio show on Radio Kwizera and were motivated by what we were doing. At the time we didn't realise how powerful our radio show was – the reach that it had. Every Sunday people tuned in to listen to our show: in Tanzanian refugee camps, in Tanzanian villages and also in non-refugee communities bordering Tanzania in Burundi, Rwanda and the DRC. Our show was broadcast into Tanzanian homes and beyond.

Many parents recognised the importance of our show and then allowed their children to participate in the Child Voice Out Campaign, Children's Parliament, sports activities, the radio show and other workshops and training that my colleagues and I conducted. We could feel their happiness and the support they provided; they were proud of us as children of Lugufu. We could feel how much they believed in us.

It was at this time that I became very busy and my schedule was full. I was the head of the programme and also the radio show presenter. I introduced the topic to listeners and moderated the entire show, calling on others to give their inputs on the topic. In the beginning it was a little difficult because I had to grow my capacity to speak, think and reason. I learnt how to lead a conversation, ask questions, introduce other opinions and make suggestions about the topics under discussion.

Some villagers told me: Baruani, since my daughter started coming to your workshops she is confident, speaks up and offers advice, something she would not do before. You guys are doing a good job!

I was happy to hear these comments coming from parents. I became well-known all over the camp and people gave me the nickname 'Mtoto Wa Afrika' (Son of Africa). I travelled to different villages, attended gatherings and spoke to the communities about children's rights. I had found my purpose. I had found my voice.

In 2008 I was in Grade 8. A typical day looked like this: I woke up early in the morning and got ready for school. Then I attended school. After school I'd do some work at home, check my homework and in the early evening go play soccer. If I had meetings I would rest a while and then prepare for the meeting or workshop. My plans changed every day, depending on what I had to do.

As Chairman of the Children's Parliament and presenter of the radio programme, I participated in all meetings organised by our representatives from the school committees and gender-based violence groups. I also had to rehearse with the 'Sisi Kwa Sisi' team for each new radio programme. I tried to fit everything in – my life was busy.

I was involved in almost all the weekly radio shows as head of the programme and the presenter. Sometimes my deputy stood in and with some of the topics we invited special guests to clarify and speak on certain topics and also respond to questions from the children. In this way we helped each other, preparing the topics, posing some questions and planning how we would run the entire show. Together.

This is how I became an activist.

CHAPTER 6

MOVING TO NYARUGUSU

The decision to close Lugufu Refugee Camp was made by the Tanzanian government and the UNHCR in an effort to accommodate refugees better; a decision that was implemented after a meeting with refugee leaders.

Our leaders wanted to know why the camp was being closed and what the closure process would look like. They had an opportunity to speak but I'm not sure their voices were heard. It made no difference. The Children's Parliament was informed through our supervisors that we would all be moving to a new refugee camp: Nyarugusu. There was no consultation with us. We were made to understand that sometimes refugees are not regarded as people who need to be consulted about decisions affecting their lives. We were told what was going to happen and had to follow instructions.

The UNHCR and Tanzanian government representatives merely told us that they were closing one Congolese refugee camp. We were shocked because it happened so quickly. In a few months we were expected to be ready to leave. Bibi was confused as Lugufu had become home to us. We were being forced to move and start over again. It was unsettling and painful.

Only two refugee camps would remain in Tanzania: one for Congolese (Nyarugusu) and one for Burundians (Mtendele). The reason given for the move to close our large refugee camp and place all DRC refugees into one camp was to make it easier. One camp was easier to manage than two camps. But it was not easier for us. At the time there were more than thirty thousand DRC refugees in Lugufu and at least that many in Nyarugusu as it was a bigger camp.

There were multiple refugee camps in Tanzania when I first arrived in 1999. Ten years later in 2009 only three refugee camps remained: two for Congolese refugees and one for Burundian refugees. And now it was being reduced to two camps. There were two options presented to us as refugees living in Lugufu: voluntary repatriation back to the Congo or get ready to move to Nyarugusu. We would be informed about the process of moving to Nyarugusu by our zone and village Leaders. Done.

As soon as our leaders received information from the authorities they shared it with the rest of us at village meetings. Ahead of these meetings the village leaders walked through the entire village with a microphone, calling everyone to attend a meeting the next day at the village square. Villagers were told about the move to Nyarugusu camp and were shocked. Some of them were still busy building their first houses and now being forced to move to a different camp was distressing, Many were devastated and couldn't believe what was happening to them. Again.

I only had one option …

I had to move to Nyarugusu because my adopted family wasn't ready to go back to the Congo and I also had nobody else to live with and nowhere else to go. I was still a minor, an under-age child at the time, and moving to Nyarugusu was my only, and best, choice.

I asked myself many questions, all the time, about what was happening in my life. I was dependent on other people's decisions. I had been living with this stress for years. Not knowing the whereabouts of my loved ones, missing them all the time, feeling I had no power, wondering where I belonged.

Three months later the move to Nyarugusu started. Thirty thousand refugees from Lugufu packed up their belongings, hoping to find more permanent homes in this new place. We gave up much: homes we had built with hope and love, small vegetable gardens that put food on our tables, a safe and trusted community where children played, homes where we had started feeling safe…

Each zone gathered in a specific location where departure information was given. When our zone's turn arrived the family heads went to the allocated area to confirm the names of all their family members and they then received a departure date. It all felt so familiar …

To see everyone pack up and leave was emotional. Families packed up their belongings to be ready for the trip. The process of rehousing refugees started in September and ended in December 2009. Lugufu and Nyarugusu camps were both in the Kigoma region but in different districts: Lugufu was in the Uvinza district and Nyarugusu in the Kasulu district with a distance of 220km between them. Because of rough country roads it took us eight hours to get to Nyarugusu.

Again we travelled in UNHCR trucks with approximately fifty people on each truck. There were few seats and these were reserved for the elderly, pregnant women, people with disabilities and children. The rest of us stood for the whole journey. All eight hours. We stopped at a village called Kasangezi, 72 km from Lugufu, where we rested, ate and went to the bathroom. We saw many Tanzanian villages on the way from Lugufu to Nyarugusu camp. When we passed by villagers sitting on the roadside waved at us as they sang. We could feel the love they had for us even though we were refugees.

I was sixteen and in charge of managing our family's luggage, both before leaving and also after arriving. At this time I was widely recognised because of my role in the radio show and Children's Parliament. Sometimes those who did not know my face realised who I was after I introduced myself. As a result I was able to ask people who were assisting us for help in finding our bags. I also asked them for a speedy allocation of our plot where we would build our new house. This was the best moment with my adopted family because they could see my contribution was valuable and everyone was grateful to have me help in this way. My relationship with my adopted family was good at this time. We arrived in Nyarugusu in September 2009.

Things were different this time. When we arrived in Nyarugusu each family was given four hundred bricks to build their house. Everyone got the same number of bricks irrespective of how large the family. Pots, plates, spoons, forks and blankets were given according to how large the family was.

And life started again.

Things were also a bit different because we built our homes on empty plots in between existing houses, alongside refugees who already lived in Nyarugusu. Some refugees from Lugufu were placed close to their old neighbours while others were taken to new villages and had to make friends with new neighbours. Our neighbours who were already settled in Nyarugusu supported us a lot in building houses. Some shared their homes with their new neighbours, while helping them to build their new homes. We were not able to get a place to stay as our family was big so we built temporary tents. With the support of our neighbours we made extra mud bricks, built our houses and moved in a few months later. People supported one another. Men and women worked together to build their homes, going to the forest to cut grass for the roofs. My entire family helped to make sure that the houses were ready to live in as soon as possible.

The start of the DRC academic year was September, the same month we arrived in Nyarugusu. It was a difficult time for all refugee children still attending school. Some children could not attend school at all until they had helped their families build their new homes. Others, like me, often missed school during the week because we had to make bricks and search the forest for grass for the roof. I was sometimes late for school but also missed many school days entirely. I continued my work doing family chores after school but also tried to make time to carry on with my children's rights' activities. There were girls in our family but as they were still young we boys had to do domestic chores: fetch water, firewood and do the cleaning. These were some of the main chores I had to do at home each day.

This was a really tough time, not only for me, but also for all the re-housed families. We were exhausted and needed time to rest. Like the way we used to in Lugufu.

Our children's rights activities started drawing attention again. We had arrived in a big new community where many did not know what we had done in Lugufu. Our new community members were impressed and again we received congratulations from refugees living in Nyarugusu and even from citizens living outside the camp.

We were reaching many more people now than in Lugufu because the community was bigger and we had to include more refugee children from Nyarugusu. It was important to include everyone, make the activities belong to all of us, from both Lugufu and Nyarugusu, without excluding anyone. Our programme activities helped many children learn about children's rights.

We had education-related discussions to ensure all children of school-going age were allowed to go to school. Our discussions also showed that all children have the right to health, the right to play and freedom of expression. Through these discussions children were able to access these rights at school, speak to parents about them and also advocate with the authorities to build more schools so that no child was out of school. Both girls and boys: all children had to go to school.

It was easy for the Children's Parliament started in Lugufu to continue in Nyarugusu because World Vision Tanzania was in charge of child protection in Nyarugusu as well. After arriving we had a meeting with the officers previously from Lugufu and also those currently in Nyarugusu to plan the way forward. The decision was made to double the groups to include the children from Nyarugusu.

The selection of committee members was done under the guidance of our supervisors. We then had a meeting with all children, old and new, to inform them about the new group that was being formed. Now we could move forward. Every village was represented by six members, which made three hundred and six members from fifty-one villages. The group was now double the size of the previous number to accommodate children from Nyarugusu. The responsibilities were the same and everyone participated in the activities.

After the arrival of Lugufu refugees Nyarugusu camp housed more than seventy thousand refugees. This number continued to grow with almost two hundred thousand refugees now calling Nyarugusu home.

Parents wanted their kids to be part of our programmes and when our radio show started airing again people in the camp were keen to listen to the next episode, to hear the new topic of discussion. They were impressed because we were doing things as children that they expected older people to do. As children we were leading the way.

Our programmes gave children the confidence to speak about everything that was happening in their lives without being afraid. Children were encouraged to debate when they didn't agree with certain things. This was very much against our culture, as our culture does not regard children, girls and women as equals who can contribute anything meaningful to conversations. Women were expected to stay at home to cook, wash clothes, and clean while husbands went to work. Girls were expected to stay at home, work and wait to be married. Children were expected to have nothing to say until they grew up.

But we changed perceptions. Some people still did not agree with what we were doing but many were supportive because they could see how happy their children were when they were free to speak up and speak out.

All this happened before winning the International Children's Peace Prize.

That was when my life changed forever.

Yet again.

CHAPTER 7

WINNING THE PRIZE

December 3rd 2009 is a date I will never forget. This is the day I was awarded the International Children's Peace Prize by the KidsRights Foundation in The Netherlands. I never dreamed this could happen but it did and I am very happy and grateful for that.

Life is full of ups and downs and often all we need is to be grateful for every season. We should not allow ourselves to give up because if you give up once it becomes easier, eventually, to give up completely. Winning the prize was like putting fuel on the fire, it gave me a lot of energy because it made me realise that if people could recognise what we were doing that meant I needed to do more! I could see the results brought about by assuming greater responsibility. This prize gave me more responsibility which I was happy to embrace and wanted to work towards doing even more.

How did I get to win this prize? Unbeknown to me it all started when I was still in Lugufu camp. Mr Zakayo Kalebo, World Vision Programme Manager, nominated me. I had never met him before being nominated. My friends and I went about our daily activities advocating for children's rights through the various Child Voice Out campaigns like the Children's Parliament and the radio show without knowing that our supervisors were taking note of our actions and spreading the word about our work.

You will remember that at the beginning of 2009 when the UNHCR, together with the Tanzanian government, decided to close Lugufu Camp we were offered two options: return to the

DRC through voluntary repatriation or move to Nyarugusu. At that time Mr Vincent Mhangwa, World Vision community services coordinator, came to our home and requested a meeting with Bibi and me. He wanted to know whether we were returning to the DRC or moving to Nyarugusu. Bibi told him that we'd be going to Nyarugusu. He seemed delighted, saying that's what he wanted to hear. And then he left. We had no idea what was going on.

One afternoon I was walking around my village in Nyarugusu with friends and I was told someone was waiting for me at my home. I was told that he had arrived by car - you can imagine the stir it created in the camp when a stranger arrived to see you, driving a car!

I was curious to see who it was. Why was he here? What did he want from me? My friends and I ran as fast as we could. Somebody arriving to see you at your home was enough of an oddity, but arriving in a car was unheard of! Everyone in the village was curious about who had come by car and why he was there.

I thought it might be someone from a supporting organisation who wanted me to participate in a campaign or do some training. When I got home I saw Mr Mhangwa waiting for me in the car. I greeted him and he said hello back. I had seen him around the camp but had not had time to talk to him.

We smiled awkwardly at each other and I quietly waited for him to tell me why he was there. He started by acknowledging that my colleagues and I had been doing great work through the children's rights activities in the camp, something that had been noticed. I was very happy to hear this. And then he said: Baruani, I am here to take a passport photo of you – it is needed.

What?

I didn't ask why, just felt grateful to be in this favourable position where somebody wanted to take a photograph of me. He told me that my supervisors would get back to me if they needed anything else. He then left and I wished him a safe trip.

I have never forgotten this special meeting; even now I can picture it: my heart beating wildly, the confusion of not knowing why he was taking a photograph. Why was it taken and who wanted it? Every few days my friends asked me about it. I hoped that it was a good thing and was curious to know what was going on.

Bibi kept asking me if Mr Mhangwa had told me anything since taking the photograph. No. Then she said: OK, let's wait. They will come back to us when they have something to say.

Life in Nyarugusu continued as usual. I had a good relationship with everyone at home. Everyone was keen to know what was going on. The family congregated around the fire at night where we sat and spoke about family matters, mostly in the evening after eating.

All my friends from Lugufu had moved to Nyarugusu, along with all the Children's Parliament members. Before we left Lugufu we had a final meeting with all the Children's Parliament members regarding the way forward when we arrived in Nyarugusu. Our child protection supervisors told us that everything was in place, they were in touch with their colleagues in Nyarugusu about how to implement the programmes as soon as we arrived. Because everything was in place we were able to meet at the Child Protection Offices a week after we arrived to kick-start the programme with the Nyarugusu children joining the activities. It was not easy because we were all busy sorting out our family matters: building houses, enrolling in schools and then fitting in the meetings too. We tried our best to do it all and, to a large extent, succeeded. The supervisors who had been working with us in Lugufu continued to work with us along with supervisors from Nyarugusu. A new, bigger team was formed.

And then, for the first time, I met Mr Zakayo Kalebo, WVT Kigoma Programme Manager. I finally met him two months after moving to Nyarugusu, more than six months after my passport photo was taken.

He asked me: Baruani, are you ready? I responded: Yes.

He asked again: Are you sure? I responded again: Yes.

Without knowing what it was about, he hugged me and left.

I had no idea what was going on. I thought maybe he was asking me about my daily activities in the camp. I couldn't sleep that night. It was unsettling being asked such a weird question by someone in his position. It weighed on my mind and I could think of nothing else. Even so, I continued with my daily activities as usual.

A few days later, during our weekly meeting our child protection officer joined the meeting because she wanted to share some news. She revealed that I had been nominated for a big prize, the International Children's Peace Prize, awarded by the KidsRights Foundation. And if all went well, I would be travelling to The Netherlands to receive the prize.

From the time of being nominated it took almost nine months to receive confirmation that I was the winning candidate from over a hundred nominees from many countries all around the world. I had won the 2009 International Children's Peace Prize!

I couldn't believe it and started crying in front of my friends. It felt like a dream, not real. Everyone was ecstatic because this was a victory for the collective work done by each one of us in the group. This was a sign of the power of the work we were doing and was just what we needed to fuel our activism. We were all from different families but had the same goal: advocating for the rights, not only of refugee children, but also for all children, wherever they lived.

We were many individuals with one mission.

We came from different, challenging situations and wanted to prove to ourselves (and others) that it doesn't matter where you come from, whether you are rich or poor, white or black: one person can make a difference.

I told my friends: This is our prize; we should be proud of ourselves and we need to stick together. We deserve each other and we must work together to bring more positive change to our families, communities, country and the world at large.

After the meeting, the child protection officer said she would get back to me soon for more updates. A few days later it was confirmed in writing that I was indeed the 2009 International Children's Peace Prize winner.

It was the best moment of my life.

I can't express how happy I was. Some of my friends came over to congratulate me but I kept telling them: Guys, this is not about me alone - this is the result of working together, Yes, I am the winner but this prize belongs to all of us. It is through our determination that we are here today. We shouldn't look down on ourselves.

Everyone at home was happy, dancing and singing for and with me. It was a glorious moment. Bibi was so proud of me. She told me: I can't believe you could do something like this. It started like a movie and look where it is taking you now.

So many questions, one being: How is it possible for a refugee like me to win this prize?

Considering my life in the refugee camp and then hearing that I had been nominated for and won an international award was mind-blowing. One affirmation which I still claim today is that it doesn't matter who and where you are, everything is possible and comes at the right time. It's a truth I still claim.

And then I started worrying about all the challenges involved. As a refugee, I had no passport which allowed me to travel. How was I going to get to The Netherlands? I left this admin to others and moved on to other things that were also important to me; things that I worried about regarding going on this trip to Europe. I was happy and worried at the same time. Imagine travelling from Nyarugusu, a refugee camp in East Africa, all the way to Europe.

It felt like a miracle.

I learnt again that it is possible to have conflicting emotions at the same time. Some things that I worried about:
Flying in a plane: From the time I was born to the age of sixteen I never thought of or even dreamed of flying in an aeroplane. So I had no clue what would happen. I had seen people travelling by plane in movies but I did not know if the movies were portraying something real or if it was just fantasy. Happy and

worried, I imagined being in the sky. I couldn't believe I was flying in an aeroplane. I was nervous because, while in the sky, I couldn't imagine looking down. Was this really happening?? Or was I dreaming?

Travelling outside the country and leaving the African continent: This was not every day travel, merely leaving the camp. This involved leaving the Kigoma region, going beyond the borders of Tanzania, saying goodbye to the African continent. You can imagine that travelling for the sake of travelling was already an adventure for me. I felt like a full human being for the first time. This might seem unbelievable to many but it was a big thing for me. The biggest thing that I had ever experienced. Watching football on television in Tanzania had me thinking that this was real: I would be travelling to a place we had seen on television, a place which previously had seemed beyond my reach. I wondered: would it be possible to go watch a football match in a stadium, especially my favourite team, Chelsea? I had never dreamed of seeing my favourite players that I'd been cheering for on television for all these years. Unfortunately I did not get the opportunity to go see a soccer match but I was taken to Ajax Football Club stadium in the city of Amsterdam. No match - just the stadium. And it was thrilling!

Food. This was something that I knew for a fact would be complicated because I had grown up in a place where I ate the same food every day: 'pap' with green / yellow / red beans, meat, fish, cassava and potato leaves. So, what types of food do people in The Netherlands eat? Would it be the same? How was I going to cope and would I enjoy their food? I realised eventually that every new moment you face in life is the start of learning new experiences. I was ready to enjoy new food options. When I arrived in Amsterdam I had to find a way to embrace this new food journey. My solution? I put sugar on everything except fish and meat! Sugar had never been part of the food issued to us – ever – and I discovered that I loved it!

My hosts were astonished (and maybe a little perplexed!) at how I was sprinkling sugar on everything. They were very accommodating until I tried to put sugar on a pizza - that was a step too far! But it was my mission to enjoy Dutch food, a scary new experience. Ninety percent of the food I ate in the Netherlands was new to me. Some things I sampled that I had never eaten before: pizza, pancakes, burgers, cheese, and so much more. The only thing that I didn't like eating was cheese; I didn't like the taste. Often Dutch meals involve bread and that was something I thoroughly enjoyed.

Language is the most important thing in life. If you don't understand one another or speak the same language your ability to communicate is limited. Language has always played a big role in my life. I wondered how I would communicate and interact with people in The Netherlands because I knew for a fact they would not understand my home language. I speak fluent Kibembe (my mother tongue) and Swahili. I was in Grade 8 at the time so I could speak a little French as well. I was worried about how I was going to communicate with them as I knew no English? I was terrified but had no other option than to wait and see what would happen.

At the beginning of October 2009 it was again confirmed that I had won the 2009 International Children's Peace Prize and World Vision Tanzania started preparing all the documents needed by the Tanzania government as well as The Netherlands Embassy to get a permit to leave the camp and acquire a visa to travel to Europe.

I met Mr Kalebo at the Head Office in Kasulu where I was told what the process was and how long it was going to take to get everything done. Mr Kalebo told me that three of us would be travelling to The Netherlands: him, Vincent Mhangwa and me. At that time, they were hard at work getting all the required documents before going to Dar Es Salaam to apply for the travel document that would allow me to travel abroad. Once I had a travel document I could start the visa process. I was happy to hear that.

Although I was looking forward to the trip, I was also worrying about the obstacles preventing me from travelling. Be calm. Wait. It's happening ...

It was a long, complicated process for a refugee to leave the camp, let alone the country. Various departments inside and outside the camp were involved. World Vision Tanzania had to send a letter to the Ministry of Home Affairs and copy UNHCR for the issuing of a permit letter for me to leave the camp. Before leaving the camp I had to report to the Nyarugusu police station to inform them that I had been granted a permit to leave the camp for a certain period, as written in the permit. In total four departments were involved for me to leave the camp: World Vision Tanzania, Police, UNHCR and Home Affairs (Refugee Department). The process to be granted a permit did not take too long.

And then it was time to travel to the capital city to apply for my travel document (a refugee's 'passport') and visa to travel to The Netherlands. We travelled by car from the camp to Kigoma where we took a flight to Dar Es Salaam. I couldn't believe I was boarding a plane. I cried once inside the plane because this was a dream to me.

A few hours later we arrived in Dar Es Salaam, the capital city of Tanzania. We immediately started the application process for a travel document. This was the first time I realised that there is a special Refugee Travel Document. The big difference between a refugee travel document and a citizen passport was that a travel document has to be renewed every two years while a Tanzanian passport was valid for ten years,

I was terrified that maybe I would not be allowed to travel because I was a refugee. After applying for the travel document and Schengen visa we returned to Nyarugusu.

It took a month to finalise the refugee travel document to leave Tanzania and the Schengen visa to enter The Netherlands. Before leaving the camp for The Netherlands very few people knew about the prize and where I was going. KidsRights Foundation rules stated that no public announcements were allowed to be made about who had won the prize until it was announced at the ceremony in The Hague on 3 December The WVT staff, the Child Voice Out team and the family all said good luck for the trip and wished me a safe return.

After many hours of air travel we arrived safely in Amsterdam and went straight to the hotel to rest for a few hours before starting the programme for the day.

Kidsrights Programme coordinator, Ellen, came to the Airport to meet and welcome me. It was amazing to see how beautiful and big Schiphol Airport was. I had never experienced cold like this back in the camp as we had come straight out of an African summer. We travelled with Ellen by car from the airport to the hotel. I had two bags, one with clothes and a satchel for my books. I had done some shopping in Dar Es Salaam so had a warm jacket, scarf and gloves to cover up against the cold.

I remember standing outside the hotel to experience the snow. What was this? Rain? Salt? What exactly?

It was amazing!

The only person from KidsRights I knew was Ellen so I looked forward to meeting the entire team. I was happy being in that big city and was being looked after so well. We had a special driver who took us to different places during our stay.

The next day or so I was taken to different places to see how big and beautiful The Netherlands was, especially the capital city, Amsterdam. I travelled on water canals and viewed old historical buildings. I went to Anne Frank's house, Amsterdam Central and other places and was amazed to see so many strange things. In a way I was jealous to see how beautiful this country was compared to the bleakness of the refugee camp where I came from. It was a shock comparing Nyarugusu to Amsterdam.

Mr Mhangwa, my interpreter, translated everything from English into Swahili. He made communication possible during our stay and I truly appreciated him for this. It was, however, challenging not being able to speak English myself as it definitely created a barrier. People like communicating directly so speaking through an interpreter made things awkward. We had no other choice and he helped me a lot.

I did multiple interviews with local journalists and international radio and television presenters before the ceremony, speaking about the work my team and I had been doing in Tanzanian refugee camps. They wanted to know all about where I came from, the work I was doing in the camp and life in general. The most frequently asked question was: How did you feel when you first heard that you were the winner? This was the first question that anyone asked me, from my friends to everyone I met. It was a busy time which was good because I loved speaking about our work.

The ceremony was held in The Hague in a parliament building called the Hall of Knights. This historic building is one of the oldest buildings in The Netherlands. The Hall of Knights is very beautiful and when I arrived I couldn't believe my eyes. I wanted to see what it looked inside and was taken to all the rooms to see the beauty of the building.

I was taken into a side room where the Prime Minister, Mr Jan Peter Balkenende, congratulated me ahead of the ceremony. After speaking together for almost ten minutes he gave me two gifts: the first was a T-shirt from the Netherlands football legend, Johan Cruyff, and the second one was a very beautiful Michael Kors watch. In the photo taken on the day you can see that I was extremely happy! I was also a little overwhelmed. I felt as if I was in heaven. I even almost forgot that I was a refugee from Tanzania!

That day, 3 December 2009, my life changed as I walked in procession down the long aisle on the red carpet with hundreds of applauding people standing, welcoming me, celebrating me. That day I started yet another life journey.

The Prime Minister of the Netherlands, Peter Balkhenende, and Marc Dullaert, Founder of KidsRights Foundation, led the way. I followed them. There were hundreds of people in the Hall of Knights. It was a formal gathering of government officials, officials from various organisations and diplomats. Wangari Maathai, winner of the 2004 Nobel Peace Prize, was the guest of honour who handed over the trophy to me. The International Children's Peace Prize (ICPP) is awarded annually to a child who fights courageously for children's rights. This prestigious youth prize was launched by KidsRights during the 2005 World Summit of Nobel Peace Laureates in Rome and the prize is always handed over by a Nobel Peace Prize laureate.

My speech that day was about the work that I was doing in the camp.

"Circumstances in the refugee camps are poor and growing up in a refugee camp means growing up without a future. There are shortages everywhere. But the worst thing is growing up without a future. It is my greatest wish that through radio, children all over the world will raise their voices and speak up so that their rights will be respected everywhere."

My entire speech was in Swahili because I knew no English at the time. Sub-titles enabled the Dutch audience to understand what I was saying. Before going on stage they played a video which showed where I came from and the work that I was doing in the camp.

I could see how touched the audience was while delivering my speech and after the ceremony a lot of people came to congratulate me and wish me well. After the ceremony we went to another beautiful room for dinner. Some people wanted to know more about my life in the camp and how I came up with the radio show idea. The food was good but I struggled to eat. As there was no sugar around I couldn't sprinkle sugar on my food. And so I didn't eat!

After a whirlwind week in The Netherlands we returned home to Nyarugusu, To Africa. To summer.

Even though I loved the Netherlands and wished that I could live there I was happy to get back in Nyarugusu. Some refugees in the camp had learnt about my winning the International Children's Peace Prize on the radio through the interview I did with BBC Swahili. It had also been officially announced by World Vision that a refugee boy had won the International Children's Peace Prize as a result of the incredible work done by him and his friends in advocating for the rights of children. From that point onwards everyone in the camp knew about it and those who had never met me before wanted to meet me. In this way my team and I became even more popular within the camp and across Tanzania.

Public reaction after winning the prize was heart-warming and the work that my team and I were doing through the Child Voice Out campaign, sports initiatives and the Children's Parliament was more widely recognised. The radio show 'Sisi Kwa Sisi' was broadcast to neighbouring countries with many people wanting to know more about this young refugee boy. Many people came looking for me, some people not only wanted to see me, but they also came especially to congratulate me and my friends for the work we were doing.

When I got back home after the ceremony there were acts of jealousy from some children and some elders as well. It was difficult for them to accept that one day we are all the same as refugees and all of a sudden one of us travels to Europe and then comes back to the camp changed because of the experience, no longer the same. I faced a lot of pressure because there were expectations created by my visit to Europe. Some people thought I had received a lot of money and I should share it with them. When I tried to explain that I had come back home with nothing many people simply did not believe me. This created problems. Some parents were jealous because they believed that their children should also have been acknowledged. It wasn't easy to return home with nothing but memories.

I came home with the International Children's Peace Prize trophy called the Nkosi (named after Nkosi Johnson, a young South African HIV/AIDS activist, the first winner of this international award). It also came with a prize of hundred thousand Euros, a grant that supported projects aligned with the work I was doing. It was used to support refugee children's education in the camp by building libraries and an internet café. In this way, children in Nyaragusu had more access to reading materials and a better knowledge of what was happening in the outside world. These projects were administered by the various support organisations in the camp and the prize money was paid to them to implement these projects,

This award helped me, together with my team, to continue advocating for children's rights more and more. And it also gave me more confidence. I haven't been the same person since winning the award.

I have nothing to give to KidsRights Foundation but I appreciate them so much for acknowledging my efforts and introducing me to the world. And the world to me. Over the years there have been some very special liaison officers who have offered amazing support and I fondly remember Ellen, Sjierly, Laura and Karin. Thank you for all the opportunities that you created for me and supporting me in reaching for my dreams.

CHAPTER 8

OPPORTUNITIES & CHALLENGES

I am grateful for the many travel experiences I've had after winning the International Children's Peace Prize. From the day I won the prize my work multiplied and I was involved in speaking at both local and international levels.

I received invitations from different organisations, through World Vision Tanzania and the KidsRights Foundation, inside Tanzania and beyond our borders. These opportunities helped me grow my life experience in different ways, especially regarding public speaking. I focused on different topics, according to the theme of the specific event. It was an honour for me, not only as a young boy but also as a refugee, to address diverse audiences: men and women, boys and girls – so many people from so many communities. I didn't 'have' to feel ashamed to tell them I was a refugee because they all wanted to know what it was like living as a refugee. All these discussions happened through speeches, debates, while on a plane, in restaurants and in malls. As a children's rights activist I was included in everything related to or involving children or refugees and every opportunity I got I made sure I represented my refugee community well - raising uncomfortable issues with world leaders - urging them to take action.

How was I treated on my travels? Quite differently in different places and spaces. Through travelling nationally and internationally I experienced and learnt so many things. I was treated with respect and dignity on aeroplanes by flight attendants as all that mattered to them was to make sure I was happy and comfortable.

Staying in hotels was sometimes a challenge. Some hotel employees, especially those who had never met refugees before, wanted me to present a typical ID or passport which I didn't have and this led to confusion. Some international hotels knew about all sorts of documents and recognised my refugee documents and responded in an appropriately professional manner.

Generally most people treated me well, whether on a plane, at a hotel, or at a conference. In general spaces people were friendly and I was treated with respect. Some people knew where I came from and wanted to know what life was like in the refugee camp, while others were familiar with refugees. Some people congratulated me for not giving up and encouraged me to continue advocating for refugee rights.

Each time I returned to the camp after a trip abroad I had many stories to share with my family and friends, things I had not imagined before. Food became part of these talks of my adventures. With the food distributed in Nyaragusu being almost the same every month and year, travelling to new places helped me to experiment with different types of food. Maize meal, green and red beans, cooking oil and soya were our usual staples. Sometimes there was also fish and meat from the market. We ate the same staples day after day, month after month, from January to December.

There were changes in my body whenever I returned from a trip to the outside because my body had to adjust to the new food on every trip. When I returned to the camp I felt a little different because my body had started adjusting to a new diet after a week or so. And then back to the staples. My favourite food from the outside world that I missed on my return to camp from my first trip was pancakes: I had tried them once and had thoroughly enjoyed them!

Refugees in Tanzania live under internal Tanzanian and international refugee laws. In Tanzania a refugee may not own or buy a parcel of land to farm or grow crops, Refugees supposedly live temporarily in refugee camps, so consequently cannot buy or own land. This is also why refugees receive food stamps from the World Food Programme through the UNHCR.

Sometimes I had a hard time with hosts because it was difficult to cope with their food. I didn't know what the food was called or what the food was made of but the taste was not familiar to my mouth! I was unable to get the exact food I ate in the camp and so slowly my mouth got used to the new foods I was forced to eat. And eventually, I started enjoying these new tastes.

Being a refugee was never anything that I felt ashamed of. Yet, at the same time, I was made to feel a little inferior as a result of the way I was treated by some people or the way some people spoke to me. People who live close to refugee camps understand the life of refugees. But there are those who have no clue about refugees. They struggle to understand us and are often not comfortable speaking to us. Some conversations I've had would blow your mind. They think a refugee is someone mentally unstable or intellectually impaired, someone who can't do things by or for themselves. An uneducated nothing who does not warrant respect and cannot be trusted. A nobody.

So many opportunities were created by winning the ICPP but it also created its fair share of challenges.

My supervisor and I once went to a hotel in Dar Es Salaam where I provided a permit letter as my ID. I was asked to provide an ID card or passport to book the room as they don't accommodate people with such previously unseen papers. I understood the receptionist had no clue concerning refugee documents. My supervisor and I had to explain in detail and assure him they could call the police to reassure them of the validity of this permit letter.

The permit letter always stated that I would be accompanied by a Tanzanian citizen to leave the camp or country. Authorities therefore always checked that the person I was travelling with was present before allowing me to enter a car or a plane. It was a must. I felt as if everything in my life depended on that person: my travel buddy; my legal companion. I wasn't allowed to go anywhere without this caretaker. I was both invisible and problematic at the same time.

I travelled with these companions for specific legal reasons but it meant so much more to me because I created a special bond with each one of them. Each relationship was different and even when they stopped working in the camp we would keep in touch. To me they were not just caretakers but more like parents and brothers; each one of them an essential part of my journey to explore the outside world. I had a great relationship with them and I have embraced their pearls of wisdom into my everyday life. At that time, I had nothing to give to them other than appreciate the time we shared.

Special times. Thank you Father Zakayo Kalebo, Edith Pagula, Vincent Mhangwa, Pancras Baguma, Danstan Makoba, Timothy Mwebe, Odas Mkondo, Arnold Kimali, Herman Dondidondi and Jessica Chirichetti. You supported me during my time in Tanzania and also when I was invited to speak around Tanzania and across the world. I have great respect for you and am grateful for you always being willing to support me when I needed you. Thank You! Asanteni Sana!

They taught me a lot, as a young man, about what I should prioritise in my life. They encouraged me to follow my dreams without forgetting to follow my goals. In life we need people who treat us as equals - we all deserve that. I did not feel as if I was travelling with caretakers but parents because no one knew they were my caretakers until I was asked by immigration officers or international hosts. They loved me and I respected them. For some of them, I was the one who made travel outside Tanzania possible, especially to Europe. But I didn't feel that I was a big deal providing a gift to them. It was only because *they* supported me that I was able to travel, explore the world and be who I am today. I should be the one thanking and praising them for everything they contributed to my life and our work; individually and collectively.

I once went to a certain Embassy to apply for a visa. I had all the required documents ready to be processed. I handed over the documents, and the assistant looked at my documents, especially the travel document, and said he had never seen this document before. He insisted I should have an actual passport to get the visa. I told him that as a refugee I was not allowed to hold a passport - it is against the law. I was asked to come back after they had consulted with the immigration authorities. After a few days, I went back to the embassy and they were then able to help me get the visa. It always took time and multiple visits to get a visa.

My stories about the refugee travel document might be repetitive but this document presented an ongoing challenge in everything I did. Every time.

In September 2019 I was part of The Chaeli Campaign delegation to Mexico to participate in the Youth Summit organised by the Nobel Peace Laureates. Yet another incident at the airport in Mexico City! All the other members of the delegation (seven of us were travelling from South Africa) went through passport control. I presented my travel document to the immigration officer who looked at it and handed it to his friend to examine. My fellow delegates were waiting for me because we were rushing to catch a domestic connecting flight to Merida. A third immigration officer arrived and asked me to follow him to a separate room where I was asked me to sit and wait. I asked what the problem was but the officer couldn't tell me. After waiting for almost thirty minutes (because he couldn't speak English) he started interviewing me through Google Translate,

He stated: I'm sorry, you are going back to Tanzania!

I argued that I had a valid Mexican visa and a South African study visa and was legally in Mexico to attend the Youth Summit. Why on earth was I being sent back to Tanzania? He took my travel document for a few minutes and eventually told me to sign a form that I would leave Mexico as soon as the Youth Summit was over. Only then was I allowed to rejoin the delegation.

I was confused and upset because I was legally in Mexico, travelling on a legal visa. This treatment remained confusing even if it was not unexpected. I was always waiting for what would happen next at airport Customs – there's always something. Over time I grew accustomed to incidents like this and just tried to remain calm and wait for the long conversation that would inevitably follow.

My friends were enraged but I told them to calm down as this was not new - I had been dealing with this kind of treatment all my life. It is what it is. I accepted and embraced these situations because they made me stronger. This is a typical example of my international travel experience. This is what happens when you're using a permit letter and refugee travel document. It's never simple.

I advocate for children's rights, both boys and girls. Our advocacy started including issues relating to women and girls' topics as well. Through radio shows and the Children's Parliament workshops we advocated for gender equality. I started getting invitations to speak at women and girl empowerment programmes at primary and high schools in the camp. I was not only advocating for children's rights but also for human rights in general. This gave me more opportunities to further research women and girls' rights. This change in my activism to support human rights more broadly created additional opportunities in my life as an activist. I believe that activism is not only about focusing on one specific task but trying to speak in different ways, as often as possible, to reach a broader audience and make a bigger difference.

If you take up the fight to be a voice for the voiceless then it is your responsibility to connect with like-minded individuals. I made sure the community knew that it is a must to invest in girls' education and that everyone should take responsibility to ensure that all girls could go to school. It was also important to advocate for the inclusion of women in various positions in the community, especially those who were suitably competent.

This shift in supporting girls' rights created some resistance in the camp because our culture does not allow a woman to engage in certain activities, so promoting the empowerment of women and girls to lead in the community was not always widely accepted. It was seen as unusual because from an early age you are taught that boys and girls are different; you are also told what women and girls may and may not do. It was difficult to convince the community to change this narrative. Even though I knew it was difficult for the community I became more and more certain that they would start to understand. My colleagues and I started a women's literacy project through which refugee women learnt how to read and write and were trained about children's rights and child protection.

In the Sisi Kwa Sisi, Radio Show we had two female assistant radio presenters: Theresa Bitche and Mary Bin July. Along our journey my colleagues and I would meet refugees who would tell us: You and your team are deceiving our girls; stop telling them to listen to you. This is against our culture!

I understood their concerns but I wanted them to know empowering someone to be capable of leading for the benefit of society is a good thing and no one should be against it.

A lot changed. Girls started to have the confidence to speak up about what they had been going through in their lives; more women stepped up and different organisations in the camp were able to support them in their empowerment journey.

As an International Children's Peace Prize winner, I was invited to speak at and attend some amazing national and international events, which included:

2009: International Children's Peace Prize: Hall of Knights in The Hague/ Netherlands
2010: Welcoming 2010 International Children Peace Prize Winner: The Hague/ Netherlands
2010: Millennium Development Goals conference: South Africa
2010: Children Radio Foundation organised by UNICEF: Kigoma, Tanzania
2010: Day of the African Child: Nyarugusu, Tanzania (16th of June every year)
2013: Youth Employment Forum organised by the Tanzania Government: Dar Es Salaam

2014: People's Postcode Lottery together with Sarah Brown (Gordon Brown's wife): Scotland

2014: ABN/AMRO Conference: the Netherlands

2014: Delegate at KidsRights Workshop Week: Amsterdam/Netherlands

2014: Delegate at Women's conference: London.

2015: Youth Summit organised by UN Youth Envoy, Ahmad Alhendawi : Amman, Jordan

2015: International Children Peace Prize Ceremony: The Hague/Netherlands

2019: WE DAY Conference where Prince Harry also spoke: London

2019: African Regional Trauma Conference: Cape Town, South Africa

2019: Delegate to Youth Summit organised by the Nobel Peace Laureates: Merida, Mexico

So many great adventures experienced in so many exciting places.

And so my world got bigger.

CHAPTER 9

LIFE INSIDE AND OUT

One hundred and fifty thousand: the actual number of refugees living in Nyarugusu Camp before I left in 2017 (according to the UNHCR). This number kept on growing, day after day, mainly because more refugees kept coming from Burundi.

Burundians started arriving in Tanzania as refugees in the early 1970s, but in 2013 the Tanzanian government closed all the Burundian refugee camps. Some were given Tanzanian citizenship while others were resettled in the United States, Australia, and Europe. The remaining Burundians were returned to their country because at that time Burundi was peaceful. In 2015 people started fleeing Burundi again because the president at the time, Peter Nkurunziza, changed the constitution, allowing him to be re-elected for a third term of office. Many citizens did not agree with his power move and this led to a civil war. As a result Burundian refugees started flooding back to Tanzania. At that time there was only one remaining refugee camp: Nyarugusu.

The UNHCR, together with the Tanzanian government, decided to open two more refugee camps, Mtendeli and Nduta, to accommodate the increasing number of refugees arriving day after day. At this stage I had been living in a refugee camp for almost twenty years so most of my life experience was that of being a refugee: school, relationships, communication and food. I had not experienced any other way of living, except that of a refugee in Tanzania, with limited memories of my childhood in the DRC.

Not a single day went by without thinking of Mama and Swedi. I wished I could share everything I had with them no matter how small. It was impossible for me to go back to the DRC because I knew nobody there and had no one to live with. I had no home in the Congo.

There have been few times where people lived in peace in the Democratic Republic of Congo. Over the past few decades people have been fleeing the country as a result of wars. From 1996 refugees from the Democratic Republic of Congo stopped fleeing to Tanzania, but it started again in 2006 and from 2009 people fled the DRC in large numbers. As a result Congolese refugees can be found in all their neighbouring countries and even in Europe and the United States.

I moved into a refugee camp as a seven-year-old and, along with all the other refugees, camp life became my everything. No refugee was allowed to leave the camp except with a special medical referral or for those in the process of resettlement. Although there were no fences in the camp refugees lived under strict restrictions not to leave the camp without a special permit from the Ministry of Home Affairs. This permit allowed a refugee to leave for a day or a week but never more than a month. There are Tanzanian citizens who work in the camp and they have a special card to ensure entry. Anyone else who wants to enter the camp has to first report to the office of the Ministry of Home Affairs in the neighbouring village to apply for a permit. Once you enter the camp you are obliged to report to the Ministry of Home Affairs at the office in the camp not only for your credentials to be recorded, but also to track your whereabouts in the camp.

Tanzanian citizens do not perceive refugees and Nyarugusu as dangerous but there are many rules restricting entry to the camp. Nyarugusu is more than twenty years old so some refugees have Tanzanian friends who sometimes come to the camp for a few days to visit and stay with their refugee friends because there are no hotels in the camp. Of course everyone enters after showing the correct documents.

Almost seventy percent of refugees in Nyarugusu camp are unemployed. It is difficult for refugees to prosper because they do not have a source of income. There are small shops inside the camp where refugees go to shop for extra stuff which they need. In these shops you can buy biscuits, body lotion, and other necessary stuff, even clothes. In a place where you have lived for twenty years, you find alternative ways of surviving. Refugees barter: exchanging food for food, 'selling' certain food products to 'buy' different types of food. No matter how seemingly small the effort, they always find a way to survive.

Some refugees have shops, restaurants, barber shops, beauty salons etc. These are small businesses which enable refugees to buy and sell amongst themselves. From my experience some refugees were trusted by certain Tanzanian citizens to sell goods for them in the camp and this is how some refugees were able to do business in the camp. Others received money through friends and family members who lived in the United States, Australia and European countries, relocated through UNHCR resettlement programmes. Wherever people found themselves, they constantly tried to exchange what they had to get money - it was difficult but this is how people tried to survive.

When starting any form of business you had to have a permit to run the business. Refugees were not allowed to own or buy a car or motorcycle or open a bank account. There were no banks in the camp. You could, however, buy a bicycle. And so most refugees walked wherever they needed to go.

Many people think that we, as refugees, have embraced our situation, agreed that living in a refugee camp is our lot in life. But we did not choose to live this way ...

The high level of unemployment among youth was one of the biggest challenges and there seemed to be nothing we could do to alleviate this situation. Statistics of the high unemployment rate showed that because refugees were not allowed to work outside the camp they were limited in terms of doing business and finding work. Every year approximately nine hundred refugees graduated from high school. There was no tertiary education in the camp which resulted in a high number of unemployed youth with time on their hands. And each year another nine hundred high school graduates joined the ranks of the unemployed.

There were small markets where Tanzanian citizens brought items to sell to refugees and some would even exchange things for different food products. Typically refugees would bring rice, meat and fish and exchange them for maize flour, green beans and soya.

Every human being on earth deserves to live in freedom. Once you have tasted freedom you realise how beautiful life is. There were times when I was allowed to leave the camp for a few weeks to attend a conference or to do training. I had to carry my permit wherever I went just in case I got stopped by police or immigration officials. Even so, just being outside the refugee control area resulted in feeling the freedom to meet new people and exchange ideas without fear of discrimination.

Intoxicating.

We all deserve to be free. Outside the camp, I felt like a proper "full" human being. When you are in the camp you don't necessarily feel hard done by because you are surrounded by people with the same status, your fellow refugees. Outside the camp I experienced different treatment; different to the treatment received inside the camp. Often it's in the small things. When people don't know you're a refugee they automatically approach you with respect, as if you are 'one of them'. The way they would talk to me, including me in their discussions, always with respect and love …

Intoxicating.

It's difficult to express fully what I mean. I am not trying to say that living in a refugee camp necessarily means that you are treated so poorly that you do not feel fully human.

No. I am trying to show that living in a camp under refugee restrictions which don't allow you to do so many things is excruciatingly different in comparison to living freely in a society where you have full rights as a citizen. Those who have lived in refugee camps might understand the point I am trying to make. Everybody on earth needs freedom of choice and movement, irrespective of who you are and where you live.

I was forced to live a small life as a refugee. After winning the prize I experienced things that I hadn't dreamed of experiencing before. I went to places where no one knew I was a refugee and nobody cared. Living in the camp sometimes makes you think that everyone knows you are a refugee. And you then feel that you are not welcome to do certain things.

Suddenly I had additional collaborators and friends and our relationships grew as we started visiting one another, inside and outside the camp.

My short visits out of the camp helped me learn things which I had never thought about, for example: shopping at a supermarket, going to the cinema, taking a taxi, ordering food from a menu in a restaurant, going out with friends to have a couple of drinks. Things ordinary citizens do every day without thinking they are special activities. All this made me feel like a 'proper' human being. I was doing things my fellow refugees in the camp could never experience. There are no supermarkets, taxis, restaurants or theatres in the camps. Just individuals and families eking out an existence, not knowing that there is so much more to life.

Children arrive in the camps at a very young age, as I did at the age of seven. Others are born in the camps. They don't know that a different life exists. How could they? They see all these things - a different way of life - on television only; and it's almost a dream, a fantasy.

When you live in an open society it helps you grow intellectually because you have opportunities to learn from others. Leaving the camp helped me to know and learn many things and a lot changed in my life. I had changed. When I was invited to speak in foreign countries I grasped the opportunity to explore these places and get to know the way people living there thought and acted.

In 2010, during the Soccer World Cup, I was invited to attend the Millennium Development Goals Conference in South Africa. During this conference I met many South Africans and while chatting with them I asked: Are there refugee camps in South Africa? The answer was "No".

What?!

Apparently South African citizens and refugees all live together, which means they share things: work spaces, schools, health clinics – and the list goes on.

Everything.

I was surprised because where I came from refugees are not allowed to live amongst Tanzanian citizens. This was the first time I heard something this beautiful and I wished every country would put into legislation laws to include refugees. I don't know why it was and still is a problem for refugees and citizens to live together in Tanzania; some say it is for security reasons. I don't agree with this statement because there are countries that don't have refugees but still have security issues. These rules and laws could and should be changed. From my experience as a refugee, I always thought refugees had to be isolated and didn't deserve certain rights. But my mind opened up to different possibilities after learning that there was a different way of doing things. I wanted everyone to know that 'refugee' is just a word but we are all human beings and deserve to be treated with respect.

I was astounded that this was possible but was unwilling to start comparing how differently South Africa and Tanzania were handling refugee issues. Each country had different immigration policies but I was honestly impressed that refugees living in SA were living in communities, not restricted to camps.

I wish every country would adopt this policy on refugees because we are all human beings and we deserve to live together and share all that we have in common.

I started seeing the possibility for a different future; the possibility for all people to live together. Eventually I started questioning government officials to see if they could do something about it. But nothing has happened, until today. Seeing the possibility of living life differently as a refugee brought a time of reflection …

We are so much more than the circumstances that led us to flee our country of birth.

I am worth more than that. And I have so much to offer.

CHAPTER 10

LEAVING THE CAMP

Leaving the camp to start tertiary study was a dream come true because I knew I was going to fight for a better future and was determined to achieve it. There was nothing that could stop me from achieving it.

I graduated from high school in July 2014 and left the camp to study in South Africa in August 2017. There are many reasons why it took me three years to leave the camp. A crucial hold-up was waiting for my final school leaving certificate which had to be issued by the Democratic Republic of Congo.

As mentioned, in Nyarugusu Congolese refugees followed the DRC academic system with teachers and everyone involved in the school system being refugees. The education system functioned with the support of the UNHCR and other organisations. But all the school documents were part of the DRC academic system. School leaving certificates were issued by the Ministry of Education of the Democratic Republic of Congo. This took a while, so I waited two years for the certificate to reach me in Nyarugusu from the DRC.

I also needed to apply for a study visa in a foreign country and for this I needed an acceptance letter from a host school. My chosen option was to study outside of Tanzania. We then researched which country in Africa would best suit my needs and why I should consider studying there. After intensive research I selected three African countries as options: Algeria, the Ivory Coast and South Africa. I chose Algeria and the Ivory Coast because French was the language of tuition. An area of concern in considering South Africa was my limited English – I spoke the language well enough but had never been taught in English. But I believed that South Africa was the best option because pursuing tertiary education in English would probably create more opportunities in the future. It was difficult to gauge how long it would take to complete my studies in South Africa but I made up my mind that South Africa was the way forward.

But first I had to get my school leaving certificate ...

I applied to education officials in the DRC to issue my school leaving certificate so that I could start the visa application process by getting in touch with selected academic institutions to see which courses were on offer. The wheels of government administration turn very slowly, especially when the request comes from outside the country with no direct human interaction. Issuing the school leaving certificate was not something that happened in a few weeks or even months, as it has to go through different departments before being approved. The International Rescue Committee and Education Department were communicating with officials in the DRC to find out how long it would take to issue my school leaving certificate. We waited and waited. And waited.

In 2015 I travelled to The Netherlands to participate in the International Children's Peace Prize ceremony and during my stay in the Netherlands I met Zelda Mycroft, mother of Chaeli, 2011 International Children's Peace Prize Winner, whom I had previously met at a Kidsrights workshop in 2014.

My relationship with Chaeli has always been good. Mother Zelda, Chaeli and I spoke about my life and activism in the camp, but more importantly my ambitions to find opportunities to study further. We spoke about the pros and cons of Algeria, the Ivory Coast and South Africa.

One of the main reasons why I decided to study in South Africa was Chaeli and Zelda (whom I now call Mom). They became my family from the start of this process so it was easy for me to decide to go live with them, because it was as if I was studying from home. This was very different from the other two options where I knew no one and coping with studying and living would be challenging. Chaeli and Mom would also help me research prospective courses and universities and prepare the documents I needed to submit the application for a South African study visa.

They started the process as soon as they got back from Amsterdam. After a while they informed me that the most important thing I needed to do, essential to start the process, was obtain the school leaving certificate. Without this I couldn't approach an academic institution, and without a letter of provisional registration I couldn't apply for a study visa.

Back to Step One.

My school leaving certificate was issued in January 2016 after many queries, reminders, letters and pleas - a process that took two years.

We could then move to the next step which was to gather all the documents needed to apply for a study visa. Many people helped me gather the documents I needed to be able to leave the camp to study in South Africa.

Introduction letters were prepared by the UNHCR and International Rescue Committee, introducing me to the Ministry of Home Affairs (Refugee Department) and later to Immigration, explaining my history and why I would be travelling to South Africa to study. Immigration had to issue the travel document enabling me to travel outside Tanzania.

Three letters of support were needed: the first from the organisation that was supporting me in Nyaragusu (International Rescue Committee) explaining that I was allowed to leave the camp and that they would ensure that I returned to the camp once I finished studying; the second from my South African host family and organisation (the Mycrofts and The Chaeli Campaign) explaining how they knew me and how they would support me while I was studying in SA; the third from my sponsor (KidsRights Foundation) explaining how and why they were sponsoring me and the full extent of their financial support of my studies and living costs for the entire study period in South Africa.

So after many months the following documents were collected and ready:
Introduction letter from the UNHCR and the International Rescue Committee
Introduction letter from Home Affairs (Tanzania)
Letter of support from The Chaeli Campaign and the Mycroft family
Letter of Support from the KidsRights Foundation
Acceptance letter from CWESI (Cape Town)
School leaving certificate from the DRC
Personal profile/biography
Recommendation letters from Desmond Tutu and Ahmad Alhendawi, United Nations Youth Envoy

After so many years of concerted effort by so many I want to express my appreciation for Arnold Kimali, Herman Dondidondi, Chaeli, Mom Zelda, Dad Russell, Karin Rozema and Carl Schmidt for making this journey finally happen, It was not easy but they stood with me to make sure that everything was possible.

My South African study visa was eventually issued in July 2017.

I started school at CWESI in Cape Town in August 2017.

My initial plan was to study at the University of Cape Town, but these plans changed soon after I arrived in Cape Town. Remember that my entire primary and high school studies were conducted in French so it was difficult to immediately start learning in English, especially at university level. I presented my academic documents to the University of Cape Town administration and they advised that I register for advanced English classes (particularly to improve my written English and reading speed) before applying for a degree at the University of Cape Town.

I was already registered at Constantia Wynberg English Shared Initiatives (CWESI), an adult learning centre, for English classes and then later at Educent. These two centres helped me grow my English proficiency by improving my vocabulary, reading for meaning and writing skills. My ability to speak and deliver speeches in English also improved. I was confidently able to participate in conversations about different topics and also defend my ideas. It took time and effort but these lessons helped me a lot.

I wanted to study as I knew that it is only through education that my life would change. I wanted to make sure I would be successful the next time I applied. I wouldn't be able to communicate in English the way I now can without the classes I took at CWESI and Educent.

My plan to go straight to university was delayed, but this detour was essential. I was at Level 2 and wanted to jump directly to Level 5 without having the necessary tools. CWESI and

Educent got me through Level 3 and Level 4 - the big gap. I do not feel bad or ashamed. It is only right to work on upskilling yourself, rather than think that you can do something while you know deep down you cannot perform at that level. After all, I only heard English for the first time when I won the International Peace Prize at the age of fifteen. I have always been patient so this was not a problem - it was what I needed to do to grow the foundation for my future academic journey.

I fled my home country, the Democratic Republic of Congo, at the age of seven and became a refugee in Tanzania. From that time I lived with the same family and my whole life was spent in a refugee camp.

And now it was time to leave them – to make a new start somewhere else - to start a new journey with unknown people and forge new bonds. Scary stuff.

Saying goodbye broke our hearts: mine, Bibi's, the entire family. This was the first long separation after being together for almost twenty years. It was unimaginable leaving the people who had stood by me through the most traumatic times of my life. They had had my back for two decades.

This was a challenging time. We had a family meeting and Bibi wished me all the best in my studies. She warned: Be careful and take care of yourself. You are going to start life away from this family so always be respectful to the people you are going to live with. You have to learn a new culture so it is your responsibility to listen and follow instructions you are given by your host. Then everything will be okay.

I could see how everyone was feeling because it was the first time I was leaving for months if not years without seeing them. Everyone was crying, including me. I knew I was going to miss my family, friends and food! But, all in all, I was happy to start this new chapter in my life.

I had to leave everything known to me, my safe space, to embrace a better life.

Equally terrifying to leaving my known family was going to live with another family, not only unfamiliar but also a white family. Can you imagine spending years in the refugee camp knowing one family with the same culture and habits and then leaving to live with a white family in a foreign country with equally foreign customs and a totally different way of living?

I was happy for the new adventure but, to be honest, living with a white family in the same house loomed large ahead of me as I left everything and everybody I knew behind and travelled into a future that held much promise, but also so many questions.

Would they accept me? Would I understand them? What would they eat?

My greatest fear was how I was going to cope living with a white family, especially in terms of cultural differences, food and just general everyday life. What would happen if I did something wrong? How would they react? Would they tolerate it, would they accept living with me and me living with them? Would it be okay if we did not believe the same things?

Breathe ...

I told myself that everything would be okay.

In August 2017 I arrived in Cape Town ready to start my new life. I started attending evening classes at CWESI (Constantia Wynberg English Shared Initiative) to improve my English in order to apply for tertiary education. CWESI is located at Wynberg Boys' High School where I was also working as an intern, to improve my English and also start to understand this new system of school education. I have so much gratitude for Wynberg Boys' High School management under the leadership of the headmaster, Jan de Waal, who gave me the opportunity to be part of the WBHS team. It was a new place and a very different environment compared to the life I had lived in the past. I was there not only to learn but also to grow a network, share my story with students and teachers and participate in school activities.

Wynberg Boys' High School is one of the best high schools in South Africa. I spent two years there as an intern but it felt like ten years. At first it was difficult because I was struggling with English and I doubted myself. Was I going cope at this school? Would the teachers and students treat me poorly because of my lack of English? The headmaster encouraged me to feel at home as I was there to learn and create relationships. He said I should not hesitate to reach out to him with any problems.

I sat in on classes and listened to what the teachers were teaching. At the same time I did various administrative tasks, assisting teachers with printing copies of exams, tests and other materials. After proving that I was ready to learn and serve at the same time, I was assigned another task at the school - to assist in the school library, making sure all the books were properly catalogued and keep track of headphones and other library materials on loan to students doing assignments. Sometimes I also supervised chess competitions. This was a good opportunity for me because communicating with so many people every day resulted in making good connections with teachers and students and my spoken English improved. All things that I needed. At some point I was also asked to be the assistant coach of the U17 soccer team, which I really loved.

I also enjoyed attending the Grade 9 camp to Grabouw and teaching Grade 8 students about children rights and the importance of education, while sharing my own journey. All these opportunities were given to me because I respected the rules and regulations of the school and was ready to learn.

I did not take it for granted.

This was a very happy time and I enjoyed being part of the WBHS school staff. I learned a lot and it gave me a sense of belonging that I so desperately needed.

Until today I still appreciate every opportunity that was given to me by the school management because it helped me to grow psychologically and intellectually.

CHAPTER 11

A NEW LIFE

I have never lived with white people before, I have just met them at conferences, workshops and other meetings. Living with them 24/7 in the same house was a scary proposition. From my learnt reality black and white people do not share a lot in common from a culture, tradition and lifestyle perspective and, possibly most important to me - the most difficult thing, food!

I was accustomed to a limited selection of food in the camp and so was asked by friends: What will you eat in South Africa? Will you get the same food that we eat in the camp?

After a great deal of worrying and thinking about food, I decided to let it go and prepare myself for what would be presented - simply open myself to enjoying new things. Easier said than done!

This was not my first trip outside Tanzania, but this leaving was different. I was leaving a country where I had lived for almost twenty years to start a new journey in a totally different country. It was an emotional time for me.

On the plane I was excited and afraid. I was starting over in a completely different environment; starting a new future. I loved the camp but it was time to move on ...

And so, after three years of sustained effort from so many, I arrived in Cape Town ready to start a new life.

I travelled with Herman Dondidondi, whose mission it was to ensure a smooth transition for me from leaving Tanzania to settle in South Africa. Kidsrights Foundation provided funds, allowing him to accompany me to Cape Town. He only stayed for five days then returned to Tanzania. But he made sure that I arrived safely with my new family and also advised me not to distract myself and always focus on the goal of why I was there.

A week later I started attending English classes to get ready for university at the beginning of the following year.

There were things I had never experienced before which made me unexpectedly very happy. Although I was an intern learning English and a new way of life, I was regarded as an educated person who had something to contribute. Imagine leaving life in the camp and ending up in a place where people wanted to hear my story and wanted me to share it with the school. I was very happy.

A few weeks after arriving I opened a bank account to manage the limited funds I had to support my daily needs. It was the first time I had spare cash to buy personal items like deodorant, body lotion, chocolate, pay for a hair-cut and order an Uber or Bolt to go and see a friend. A new life was opening up ...

Opening a bank account was an epic thing for me because having grown up in the camp money was scarce and refugees were not allowed to have a bank account. In fact there were no banks in the camp! Opening up my own account in order to manage the monthly stipend provided by Kidsrights Foundation was a huge step. It made me sad to realise that this is something my friends in the camp do not know about and will never experience.

Let's talk about food, especially pap. Pap is not just a food form to me, but something that I have a strong relationship with. Pap is what I call food, everything else is called by its name. Fish is fish, beans are beans, chicken is chicken. But pap is food. It is the staple that keeps us alive, the mainstay of our lives.

The day after I arrived in Cape Town I was taken to the University of Cape Town to visit the campus in the morning. On our way back we visited Chaeli Cottage, Chaeli Campaign Headquarters. It was lunch time and I was offered food: macaroni and cheese. I had no idea what this was and why I should eat this because it was not food. I was hungry and in need of proper food. I refused to eat it because where was the pap and meat, fish or beans? I had been told I was getting food. I was confused and started asking myself: How would I survive - would I die from hunger? Everyone at the office was confused and shocked because they couldn't understand why I refused to eat. Mom asked someone to take me to Kentucky Fried Chicken to buy chicken, something I was accustomed to eating.

Dondidondi was like a brother, making sure that I was okay. He explained to Mom the relationship
I have with food. And that this foreign macaroni and cheese was definitely not food to me! Everyone who was there that day still remembers this episode and we now laugh about it.

For the first few days after I arrived in my new home I was not completely at ease. It was difficult for me because it was a moment of trying to cope with my host family's lifestyle; everything was a new routine: eating, sleeping; interacting.

Some new tastes that I sampled in those early days included cheese, strawberries, cheese cake (which I put in my soup!) and mushrooms. I did not know what these things were called and I struggled because I was eating something that was not familiar to me. But I had to try new things and I knew my body would catch up with the new flavours and textures at some stage. I still don't like cheese, though!

I had to learn things like leaving the phone in my room while sitting with the family on the Stoep (verandah), switching off lights when leaving the room, not drinking beer in my room while others were socialising on the Stoep. These small things helped me connect with the Mycroft family.

The Stoep was a very beautiful place for me, This was Dad Russell's special place every evening, This is where we gathering as a family to braai, eat and drink. But, more importantly, it was the place where we gathered to share our stories. Everyone shared whatever they wanted to: sometimes there were serious discussions, debates and defending of arguments, but there were other times of great hilarity and funny stories. The Stoep was the heartbeat of the home, a happy place. I really loved to sit on the Stoep.

I had come from an environment where I was expected to speak only when I was asked to. But living with the Mycroft family I was encouraged and expected to speak about anything and everything. It didn't matter whether I had been asked to or not. It was a little difficult because at the time my command of English was limited and it was not easy expressing myself in English. Only people trying to communicate in a language other than their mother tongue would be able to understand this challenge. Those first few days were the hardest for me. Many of the conversations were about everyday matters and we often spoke about my day and what and how I could get the most out of the learning experiences at CWESI and WBHS.

I appreciate the guidance and advice I got from Mom and Dad. As soon as they saw me doing or saying something that was not appropriate in a particular circumstance, they would explain in a way that I could understand how to consider doing things differently for the changed environment in which I found myself. How I could do things differently the next time.

In the first weeks after arriving I wasn't mixing with anyone at home. I would put on my headphones to listen to music, I chatted on the phone while I was in the company of the family at home, in the car or basically everywhere. This one specific day Mom offered a piece of advice that has stuck in my mind and I will never forget it. She said: Baruani, it is through connecting and talking with people that you will learn to understand and speak any language. It doesn't matter what you are talking about, just talk and ask questions. Good things will come from these conversations. I follow this advice until today.

I am by nature a people person and I like having conversations and sharing my opinion. I believe that sharing opinions helps educate or inform others and in the same way I can learn by listening to their views. And being encouraged to express my views (especially differing views) was refreshing. When I was in Nyarugusu the situation was different. In Tanzania the laws and policies that govern refugees restricted us from doing certain things. And when it came to sharing opinions refugees were discouraged from speaking up and speaking out. Even when what you were thinking was positive you felt it safer to keep your ideas to yourself. So life in Cape Town and on the Mycroft Stoep was a totally different form of education. Open sharing of opinions was something which impressed me and made me content. I felt seen.

I had the opportunity to meet and interact with new people at the annual Golf Day and various other Chaeli Campaign functions. I was invited to attend leadership workshops with two different groups at Chaeli Campaign leadership workshops and I was happy to participate because I could share my story and the story of my activism from when it started until that time. This was a way in which I could continue my activism and I was excited about it.

I found that I had a talent for running. This was a new discovery as previously I considered running to be a way of leaving point A to get to point B. Or something I did when playing football. It was never running for the sake of running and the thought of a marathon seemed absurd. I joined the Chaeli Sports and Recreation Club (CSRC) and happily started participating in various races. Running in club colours was a beautiful thing because people recognised you through your club colours and you were automatically part of the team. I had to buy special running shoes because apparently you can't use just any shoes for running, there are special shoes for that! It all seemed so strange. And also wonderful. And it turns out I was good at it, which made me happy!

I entered many different shorter races and half marathons as a member of the CSRC: like the Cape Marathon, Winelands Marathon and Cape Peninsula Marathon, to name a few. Through all these activities I met and got to know new people - something I appreciate because every action, every chat, every conversation, has grown me.

I went to so many places and was able to start a new routine, a new life. Attending regular English classes became an important focus. Leaving the camp presented opportunities to move freely and nobody asked for my permit. As long as I was in South Africa legally I had nothing to worry about and nobody targeted me as a refugee or a foreigner.

My definition of the place we call home is that home is the place where you are free. And free is exactly how I felt living in

Cape Town. I was free to visit a friend; had no fear that I would be stopped by authorities and asked for my permit. The only places I was still asked for identification was at the bank and the airport, but other than that I was walking free and happy, without any fear. This changed my life. I was living in an open society, with the same opportunities presented to all community members. There were so many things I could not do in the camp which I was able to do in Cape Town. One day Chaeli and her cousin, Dylan, and I went to watch a movie in a movie house, something not really available in the camp. I enjoyed it because it was a special place to go, be entertained and refresh my mind. I also went to the Cape Town Stadium to see Ed Sheeran in concert – what a show - I enjoyed his music and this experience so much!

Being free is being active. Even psychologically, to know that I can do whatever I want to do is something which refugees in many countries do not experience. As a refugee I even limited my thinking capacity; not daring to think big or beyond my 'small' reality because I had no control over so much.

As mentioned before, living in a refugee camp your future plans are in someone else's hands. So you can have a dream but you must know that as long as someone else has to make it happen you are a long way from realising your dream. Yes, I dreamt of helping my community and later on dreamt of becoming a journalist. I knew that unless somebody helped me my dreams wouldn't be possible.

Living in community is very different to living in a controlled camp. In community you are free to do as you please, go where you want, as long as you follow the law. But in the camp everything you do is restricted - that is the law.

After living with the Mycrofts I understood that I needed to surround myself with people who understand me, are supportive and encouraging. I felt appreciated and knew my opinions were respected.

Eventually I started enjoying life in the city. I made friends at school and out of school. I was introduced to so many different people by the Mycrofts, my family. The way my role in the Mycroft family evolved could maybe be illustrated through sharing a few anecdotes that would describe my relationship with each of them …

Chaeli: Besides being my fellow International Children Peace Prize Winner, is my best friend and my sister. She has always helped me with anything I need to know, at any time. It doesn't matter if she is in a meeting, sleeping or vlogging - she always makes time to respond. I call or sms and she always gets back to me. There are no limitations regarding the topics we discuss. She has helped me deal with money management and also provides intellectual and psychological support. Chaeli has taught me a lot and still does. She was the first person who taught me how to go shopping in a shopping mall, she taught me how to use a bank card at the ATM and went to watch my first movie with me. In fact, she has been there for me from Day One. And she's still here today. She is best of the best and, as I have always said, she is my inspiration.

Mom Zelda: From the first day I met her, I knew she was a good woman with a good heart. I don't know how to describe how blessed I am to have someone who makes every effort possible to help me, no matter the cost. I can't even mention all the things she has done for me because it is a lot. Even now that I am studying she is the one providing financial support to enable me to pursue my studies. There is a lot I have not said. I have a mother who is trying her best to support me and my future. Mom doesn't take nonsense: she will tell you straight away if you are doing something wrong but also praises when you are doing right. I have been so blessed to have someone with such an open heart help and support me at every turn. In every situation that I find myself she is there - making sure I get the support I need.

Dad Russell: He passed away on 15th October 2023 at 3:35pm. He was not my biological father but he was my dad. He was a genius - I can say that. He taught me so much about electronics and the internet. Everything I needed to know I would ask him because I knew he would help me sort it out. He was a braai (barbecue) master and we would braai three to four times a week. I remember we would often sit on the Stoep chatting about football because he was a Manchester City supporter and I am a Chelsea fan. We had great football discussions while having our evening drinks: a conversation between a father and his son. For the first two years I stayed in Cape Town Dad took me to school each morning and picked me up each evening. He was a great man indeed. He never complained about taking me anywhere I needed to be. He paid for my Spotify and other stuff. I remember every time I had to fly to Tanzania to renew my travel documents he would track my plane while in the air until I reached my destination and sent a message to the family WhatsApp group.

I really miss the man. He was not only a father to me, but also a teacher, teaching me how to pronounce words the South African way: Thousands (thousands not szousands), Castle (karsil not karstil), Busy (bizzy not beezy). The list goes on – so much fun!

He always teased me about one specific incident. I was still very new in South Africa and the Mycroft swimming pool was the first one I had ever seen. I had gone for a 5km run and when

I returned I decided to have a swim in the pool. I didn't know that soap in a swimming pool is a no-no. Quite oblivious to the usual customs, I took my bar of soap to the pool, lathered my entire body and after I was good and clean I then had a swim. Dad watched me enjoy the swimming pool and later on, while braaiing on the Stoep with the family, he shared the story. We all had a good laugh once I knew that the swimming pool was not a big bath - I then knew that soap had no place in a swimming pool! Dad would tease me about this on the odd occasion and we would laugh together. I had many fabulous moments with that man; I will always remember him.

Even though we did not live in the same house, I was also part of the Turnbull family: Erin (Chaeli's big sister) and her husband, Warren and their three kids (Remy, Jon-Jon and Wells). Sometimes we would have weekend braais at their home; eating and drinking together.

A while after living with these two families I revisited my greatest fear on moving to Cape Town: how would I survive living with white people? My fear started to change and I realised that we are all human beings, able to love and protect one another. Russell and Zelda were my parents, they were my Dad and Mom and I could tell them anything without any fear because they were my parents.

I also found community in South Africa through my friend Hussein, a former refugee from Nyarugusu camp who also ended up being a refugee in Cape Town. He invited me to various Congolese and Eastern African community meetings and I realised there was quite a large DRC community in Cape Town. It was important to me not only because we are all Congolese but also, as an activist, there is much I can share with them, especially relating to children's rights. I am now part of this community and I participate in their activities.

In Cape Town I found a home, a family and a community ...

CHAPTER 12

THREE YEARS OF FIGHTING

I started using refugee-specific travel documents when I won the International Children's Peace Prize in 2009. Apart from being granted this document myself, some African heroes like Nelson Mandela were granted this document as well. In December 2013 at Nelson Mandela's state funeral tribute by President Jakaya Mrisho Kikwete, former president of the United Republic of Tanzania, he mentioned that when Nelson Mandela went to Tanzania in January 1962 he had no passport but from Tanzania he was able to travel to Accra, Lagos and Addis Ababa by means of a Tanzanian travel document. He also added that he didn't know if Thabo Mbeki had returned his, which implies Mbeki was also among those who were given the same travel document as the one I was a using.

This made me feel that I was not alone as many important people in the world had travelled this same path. I was overwhelmed at the thought.

I left Cape Town on 29 September 2019 to renew my travel document in Tanzania as it was about to expire in December 2019. This document was essential to renew my study visa. I also needed it to travel and attend conferences and workshops outside Tanzania.

I had used this travel document to attend events like the Kidsrights Peace Prize Ceremony in The Netherlands, the Nobel Summits in Barcelona and Mexico, the Women's Conference in England, the United Nations Youth Envoy Summit in Jordan (where I had delivered a keynote address), the ABN AMRO (a major Dutch Bank) Conference in

Netherlands, the WE DAY Conference in England (again as a speaker), the People's Postcode Lottery Conference in Scotland and the Millennium Development Goals Conference in South Africa. This document had served me well.

As a direct result of all the drama involved in trying to renew my travel document in September 2019 I decided to write this book because I wanted the world to know what often happens in the lives of refugees. If it is not happening to you it doesn't mean it is not happening. As previously mentioned, as a refugee my rights were often disregarded and the course of my life was in someone else's hands and there was little I could do about it.

This was the most difficult time of my entire life. I was smiling as I always do, but my heart was aching because my return to Cape Town and the future I had started imagining was dependent on getting my travel document renewed. Step One. Nothing could happen without it.

I had to return to Tanzania to renew my travel document as the Tanzanian High Commission in Pretoria could not provide clarity on whether renewing it could happen in South Africa. After multiple emails from June to August 2019 with no feedback, I decided the only option was to go back to Tanzania, as I usually do. I wanted to be in South Africa legally to continue my studies so I had to leave the country before my document expired. I had been informed by the Tanzanian Refugee Department (Ministry of Home Affairs) while still in South Africa that I had to renew my travel document. On 30 September 2019 I reported to the Refugee Department in Dar Es Salaam to start the process. I submitted all the documents to the office and was asked to return after two working days to collect the letter to take with me to the immigration office for the travel document renewal process to start. On previous occasions this process took between ten to fourteen working days.

After two working days they told me they're still in the process of speaking to Immigration about the matter and could give me no confirmation of how long this would take.

After being there for over a month I was told that passport renewal had now gone online and that no provision had been made for refugees to apply for travel documents. And now? My anguish was real.

Apparently in 2018 the Tanzanian government decided to change from biometric to electronic passports. During that period they were supposed to include refugee travel documents in the same electronic passport. Refugees were not included in the new system which made it impossible for my application to be processed. I couldn't find a refugee option to submit my details on the immigration website. This process was first implemented in May 2019. It was now November 2019.

After much back and forth the case went to the Permanent Secretary of Home Affairs and he was seemingly not aware of how refugee travel documents work. They told me to be patient, they would start working on it early in January 2020 as we were heading into the December holiday stretch.

I submitted all my documents to the refugee department of the Ministry of Home Affairs who wrote a letter to Immigration asking for more information on how a refugee could apply for a passport. After almost two weeks Immigration told the Refugee Department (MHA) to discuss how to start this process with the UNHCR because there was no way refugees could apply online. The UNHCR and the Refugee Department (MHA) started looking at whether refugee students and those going for medical treatments could travel with the former biometric passport while the government worked on including refugees on the electronic system.

This could not work because there was no way to upload or link the former biometric system into the new electronic system. All systems under the Ministry of Home Affairs had to be approved by the Permanent Secretary, there was no way any changes to the system could be conducted without his approval. The process for refugees to be included in the electronic system was difficult to approve at that time as the Permanent Secretary was a busy man.

The next alternative was to see if I could travel back to South Africa using a certificate of identity. The UNHCR wrote a letter to Immigration asking for them to issue a Certificate of Identity. Immigration informed the Refugee Department (MHA) to consult the South African Embassy to see if it was possible to travel outside the country with a certificate of identity. The answer was: No.

I was forced to cancel school for 2020 while waiting for the refugee electronic passport process to start, hopefully in the next few months, after approval by the Permanent Secretary. In March 2020 the Corona Virus pandemic erupted, with no telling when it would end. My life was on hold for the whole of 2020 with no progress made regarding acquiring a travel document. Just waiting.

From the 29th of September 2019 to January 2022 I was stuck in Tanzania with no solution in sight. The Refugee Department (MHA) wanted me to return to Nyaragusu camp but I refused and they issued a permit for me to stay in Dar Es Salaam.

What was going to happen to my studies?

What about my dream of a new life?

I was allowed to wait in Dar Es Salaam for the three years I was stuck in Tanzania fighting for a travel document to be issued. I had to report to the UNHCR Office regularly. And each time I went there was no support; all they said was that they were waiting for the government to approve the process. The Ministry of Home Affairs told me they were working on it and it had progressed to the President's office for his approval. All lies.

I knew deep down in my heart something was wrong, both from the UNHCR side and the government. Nobody wanted to tell me what was actually happening. Clearly as a common refugee I didn't have the right to be told anything. There was nothing I could do.

Back and forth between these agencies I went, week after week, month after month, for two years and eight months to be exact. This was the most emotional period of my life and it brought me to tears. I even cried in front of the authorities but nobody cared. Nothing changed. I was angry and sad. I was trying to build a future and something that had previously taken three weeks was now seemingly impossible to do. It had already stolen almost three years of my life.

During that time I lived with Wilfred Ambokile whom I had met once in 2017 through Herman Dondidondi. Once again, Dondidondi to the rescue! Wilfred gave me a place to stay and the Kidsrights Foundation supported my accommodation for the time I was stranded in Tanzania.

Wilfred and I got on very well. He treated me as his young brother; we have remained friends and are still in touch. When Covid struck I knew things would not move as expected and my heart was heavy. The unexpected thing was that there was no lockdown in Tanzania and the government was not overly concerned about Covid. People were told to wash their hands regularly and to wear face masks when visiting public offices, but that was all - no lockdown. Wilfred and I felt differently and followed the international rules from World Health Organisation. We took precautions, both in public and in private. So many people died as a result of Covid, including the President of Tanzania.

I went through a lot during those years of waiting for a travel document in Dar Es Salaam. It was emotionally and psychologically draining. Hard times. I had left in the middle of classes to renew a document and then ended up spending almost three years in limbo. It was unbelievable.

Something that could have taken a week had become a nightmare. The pandemic destroyed the country's economy and I feared that this was going to be the end of my journey. I was traumatised because there was no sign of progress. I spent much of my time reading books and watching movies, still focused on improving my English. I had financial support from the KidsRights Foundation and emotional support from the Mycrofts, my family. But I felt very isolated, alone. My life felt very hard. For almost three years I stayed in Dar Es Salaam, alone with Wilfred, away from the people I loved. Waiting for a travel document that never came.

I had family and friends in Nyarugusus, many hours away from Dar Es Salaam by road. But I knew that if I went to visit them I would never be allowed to leave, not without a travel document. And it would be more difficult fighting for a travel document from inside the camp. My safety would also be in question. Previously every time I had travelled abroad and returned to camp people expected me to have a lot of money and they would ask me for it. Obviously this was not the case – there was no cash. Now that I had been away for more than two years the expectation from people in the camp would be even higher. I couldn't trust anyone; anything could happen to me, so I had to be careful, especially when it came to protecting my own life.

In October 2021 I started playing with the idea of reclaiming my DRC citizenship and renouncing my refugee status. I had been a refugee for almost twenty-three years, since the age of seven. I had not been in my country for twenty-two years and I didn't know anyone there. But because of years of being stuck in a system that did not make provision for me and not knowing when I'd be able to continue with my studies, after almost three years of waiting, I felt it was time to be brave. I had to leave Tanzania and take the next step towards reclaiming my life.

I had a Zoom meeting with KidsRights, Mom and Chaeli and told them about my decision to reclaim my citizenship and return to the Democratic Republic of Congo. After so many years I wanted to be free and not at the beck and call of others.

I am a human being. I am an adult. I want to do things by and for myself.

The plan I had was not a simple one. I asked the Tanzanian authorities to accept my request to return to my country of birth. I knew it was the right thing to do in spite of having only a few childhood memories of the place and not knowing a single human being in the DRC.

After pushing and struggling for almost three years the time to act was now; years had gone by without a single step forward, not knowing when this issue would be resolved. It was time to do something different and make a decision to secure my future.

It was time to go back to my country of birth and claim my future as a citizen.

The idea of reclaiming my citizenship was creating a pathway to continue with my studies. I truly believe education is the best weapon to change the world. I was ready to sacrifice everything to secure a future which I believed would be better through education. I needed to get out of this stalemate situation to continue with my journey.

I went to the UNHCR office and informed them of my decision to renounce my refugee status and asked for their assistance to leave Tanzania through voluntary repatriation. The UNHCR told me if I wanted to leave the country through the UNHCR voluntary repatriation programme I had to go back to Nyarugusu to start the process from there, not Dar Es Salaam.

Yet another obstacle.

And the UNHCR had no voluntary repatriation taking place at the time. I knew if I went back to Nyarugusu I would be stuck again - l would be told to wait until the UNHCR started a voluntary repatriation drive. Only then would I be able to leave the camp. How much longer would that take?

I then informed the Tanzanian Ministry of Home Affairs that I was renouncing my refugee status. They told me to be patient as they were sure the travel document process would start anytime soon. Honestly, I was tired of the hollow promises made over the past three years! I had heard plenty of promises with no action. Eventually they told me that if I was set on renouncing my refugee status I could write a letter to the head of the department with my request. This letter would be forwarded to the Immigration Department who would then issue a certificate of identity which could be used as a passport for me to return to the DRC. A small light at the end of a very long tunnel.

And then the next step: where would I stay when I left Tanzania and arrived back in the DRC after twenty-three years, not knowing a soul? Who could help me find the information I needed and help me navigate a system I didn't know?

Of course. Dondidondi to the rescue again!

I got Mr Safari's contact from a friend of Herman Dondidondi. I had not seen my country since I left at the age of seven and I had no friends or relatives back home. This was a big challenge ahead of me. How would I cope? How could I start the process of getting my Congolese documents to apply for a passport? I had no birth certificate to prove that I was born in the DRC – did that matter?

One evening I was speaking to Dondidondi who told me that his friend, Mr Yassin, who lives in the UK, would connect me to someone in the DRC. I explained everything to Mr Yassin who then connected me to Mr Safari who lived in Lubumbashi. I told him everything that had happened to me in Tanzania and why I needed to get back home. He was empathetic and promised to help. He also told me not to worry about a place to stay - I could stay with his family until I sorted myself out.

I cried to hear him say this but was happy at the same time. All my worries disappeared and I was ready to go back home. I was ready for the next chapter in my life.

The process for me to leave the country started on the 12th of July 2022 when I was issued a certificate of identity that would expire in ten days. I had to leave Tanzania before the expiry date on the certificate.

After three years of waiting I had ten days to leave. And my life changed. Again.

Just like that.

CHAPTER 13

BECOMING A CITIZEN

I will never forget Thursday 21st of July 2022.

Air Tanzania flight number TC 213 from Dar Es Salaam (Tanzania) to Lubumbashi (DRC) through Ndola (Zambia) at 13:55 Central African Time.

This is when I arrived back in my home country, the Democratic Republic of Congo (DRC), after leaving the country twenty-three years before at the age of seven.

I was happy and yet terrified. I didn't know how I would cope, especially as I would be staying in Lubumbashi almost two thousand kilometres away from the province where I was born. I was happy to set foot in my home country no matter the consequences or challenges that awaited me. My fear was whether the DRC authorities would agree that I was Congolese, after all these years. Or they would doubt my citizenship?

I had been chatting to Mr Mlendjwa Safari, a connection of Dondidondi's, for a while via Whatsapp. He was waiting for me at the airport, ready to welcome me into his home with his family for however long it was going to take to get a DRC passport and South African study visa.

I was happy to be back in a place where I belonged. We touched down at FBM Luano International Airport in Lubumbashi and I had my certificate of identity ready to pass through Customs. I was excited and apprehensive.

Also nervous. This was the only and last option left. What if they decided to throw me out because they didn't trust me? Maybe I failed a few questions because I hadn't been in the country for so long? Imagine if they decided not to allow me entry into the country? Where would I run to? I had no passport or anything else that would allow me to leave the country. What would happen next?

On my previous travels I had entered other countries as a refugee and non-citizen of that country and they did not fully trust my intentions, so the suspicious behaviour of customs officers was justifiable in a way. My experience going back to the DRC was different. Would the Congolese customs officers accept that I was coming back home to a place I hadn't seen for more than two decades? Would I be accepted?

My turn arrived. I gave the document to the customs officer. She looked at the document and asked me: Why are you using a certificate of identity and not a passport?

I replied that I had been a refugee in Tanzania and had decided to voluntarily return home.

She responded: Ahhhh. I understand.

Her next question was: How long were you in Tanzania?

Twenty-three years, Mama.

She was shocked and felt sorry for me at the same time.

Her final words were: Karibu Ku Nyumba, Mtoto Wangu (welcome back home, my son).

I felt her warm welcome in my heart and couldn't help it. I started crying.

Tears of joy and sadness flooded down my cheeks because after twenty-three years I was again standing in the country that had taken the most important people in my life, so I cried for that.

Home, in my country of birth, for the first time as an adult.

At the time a lot was going on in my head. I was confused and didn't know what to expect next. But also I was in the DRC because I needed to get a passport in order to leave again.

On my way to pick up my bags I asked someone who works at the airport if I could use his phone to call Mr Safari who was waiting for me outside the airport.

I met Brother Safari and he took me to his house where I was welcomed with hugs from his three beautiful kids and immediately became part of the family.

Life in Lubumbashi was good. People were friendly with seventy percent of the population living in Lubumbashi being Christians. Swahili is the most popular language in the region, so it was easy for me to communicate with everyone because I speak fluent Swahili.

Mr Safari and I are from the same tribe and our mother tongue is Kibembe, I had been speaking Kibembe all these years in Nyarugusu camp as the majority of refugees were from North and South Kivu and my tribe, Wabembe, came from South Kivu. This had been a good thing because it was through my mother tongue that people could best get to know me and hear my story. The Democratic Republic of the Congo, on the other hand, is a multilingual country where an estimated total of 242 languages are spoken. The official language is French. Four indigenous languages have the status of national language: Kikongo, Lingala, Swahili and Tshiluba.

A few days after arriving Mr Safari started connecting me with people and as we were all from the same tribe we could communicate in our mother tongue, Kibembe. We spoke about so many things; about their lives, about my life. They wanted to know all about my life in the camp and how I had managed to live as a refugee for that long in Tanzania.

Have you ever experienced going to a place that you have never been before and end up meeting people who make you feel that you belong? This is what I experienced in Lubumbashi and I am extremely grateful for it.

After being a refugee for two decades returning to my country of birth is the most significant thing that has happened to me. The first thing to do was get my passport in order to get back to South Africa to continue my studies. I had to make sure everything went as planned because I had wasted three years of my life needlessly waiting in Tanzania; waiting for a travel document that never arrived. I didn't want to waste any more time.

I knew my future was at stake so I worked hard to ensure that everything happened as quickly as possible. A few days after I arrived in Lubumbashi I visited the government offices to start the application for my Congolese passport. Mr. Safari had friends who helped me navigate the government systems.

Having grown up in Tanzania I knew most of the UNHCR and immigration officers and how to work within this system. In the DRC it was very difficult because I knew nobody and the system was foreign to me. Most people my age had an ID that entitled them to vote but I had no documents at all. Mr Safari would therefore speak to the authorities and officials on my behalf first. As a citizen he had status and credibility. I spoke to the authorities afterwards. The level of corruption amongst some of these officials was significant and posed a challenge; many of them didn't care about your documents or your right to have these documents, they only cared about your money. This was very hard for me.

The only documents I had was confirmation of my high school leaving certificate. There was no birth certificate, no identity document, nothing else. I explained everything to the official and told him my full story. I even showed him information about me from the internet to prove that I was Congolese.

And then the process started. Fingerprints were taken and the passport application was submitted. One month later I got my passport!

Applying for the South Africa study visa took much longer because I needed additional documents. Six months after arriving in the DRC I left the city of Lubumbashi with my passport and study visa in hand.

At last I was ready to return to Cape Town and my studies.

A new life awaited me.

CHAPTER 14

HOME …

A heartfelt "Thank You" to Mr Safari and friends for helping me through the process of getting all the documents I needed to prove I was a DRC citizen and for making sure I got a passport so that I could apply for my study visa. I arrived in Lubumbashi at the end of July 2022 and six months later my passport and visa were ready, something I never thought could happen that quickly. I felt like crying because I had struggled for so long and so hard with no success. No matter how hard I tried in Tanzania I couldn't make it happen and, eventually, after waiting and waiting for three years, after deciding to go back to my country of birth, everything fell into place relatively easily.

How cool to be a citizen! War and conflict still today force people to leave their home countries in search of safety. But honestly, no matter where you go, home is the best.

For the first time in my life I travelled carrying not only a passport but also the confidence that comes with being a full citizen. I was keen to see how different it would be, travelling as a citizen with a passport as opposed to travelling as a refugee with a travel document.

And so I left Lubumbashi for Cape Town, South Africa, on the 30th of January 2023 at 13:45 (Central African Time) on South African AirLink Flight Number 4Z22 from Lubumbashi to Johannesburg. I arrived at O.R. Tambo International Airport and went through Customs before connecting to my domestic flight to Cape Town with CemAir Flight Number 5Z854.

Landing at O.R. Tambo International Airport and passing through customs as a Congolese travelling on a passport made me very happy. No questions at customs. I wasn't stopped. I wasn't pulled aside and roughly questioned about why I wanted to enter South Africa and how long I intended staying. I wasn't treated like a threat or a leech on society.

Nothing.

I was welcomed to South Africa.

What a unique experience - so this is what it feels like to be a citizen?

Finally ...

When I boarded my last flight from Johannesburg to Cape Town I was very happy because I was going to see Mom, Dad and Chaeli again, after such a long time away.

This is what flashed through my mind when I landed at Cape Town International Airport.

Finally ...

Six months of negotiation and reorientation in Lubumbashi. Three-and-a-half years of battling in Tanzania. Twenty-three years of surviving as a refugee in Nyaragusu.

Finally ...

At the airport I was met by my beautiful girlfriend, Feza, my sister Chaeli and Mama Zelda All of us cried. It was overwhelming to see one another again after so many years. It felt good to be back and restart my life. I was in disbelief in the car on my way back to our home in Bergvliet; I was speechless. It felt like a dream.

There were times that I had almost given up on myself but I kept moving forward. So, again, this was yet another "most important" day of my life.

When we arrived at the gate of the Mycroft home, my home, and the gate opened after three-and-a half years of being away, the word that left my lips was: Finally ...

It is true. It is happening. I am here. I am home with my loved ones.

Finally!

www.ingramcontent.com/pod-product-compliance
Lightning Source LLC
Chambersburg PA
CBHW070458090426
42735CB00012B/2601